A NUMBER OF THINGS

A Number of Things

STORIES OF CANADA
TOLD THROUGH FIFTY OBJECTS

Jane Urquhart
Illustrations by Scott McKowen

PATRICK CREAN EDITIONS
An imprint of HarperCollins*PublishersLtd*

A Number of Things
Copyright © 2016 by Jane Urquhart.
Illustrations © 2016 by Scott McKowen.
All rights reserved.

Published by Patrick Crean Editions,
an imprint of HarperCollins Publishers Ltd

First edition

Extract from "Make and Break Harbour," composed by Stan Rogers,
© Fogarty's Cove Music. Reprinted with permission.

HarperCollins books may be purchased for educational, business,
or sales promotional use through our Special Markets Department.

HarperCollins Publishers Ltd
2 Bloor Street East, 20th Floor
Toronto, Ontario, Canada
M4W 1A8

www.harpercollins.ca

Library and Archives Canada Cataloguing in Publication
information is available upon request

ISBN 978-1-44343-206-1

Printed and bound in the United States of America

RRD 9 8 7 6 5 4 3 2 1

For Sadie Jane and Rory Joseph

The world is so full of a number of things,
I'm sure we should all be as happy as kings.
—ROBERT LOUIS STEVENSON, *A CHILD'S GARDEN OF VERSES*

Introduction

A COUPLE OF YEARS AGO, WHEN PUBLISHER Patrick Crean invited me to mark Canada's 2017 sesquicentennial by writing about fifty objects, my first reaction was one of alarm. Had almost fifty years really passed since the much-celebrated centennial year, with its train whistles shrieking the first four notes of "O Canada," its hippies dressed in the new Canadian flag, its oddly shaped poured-concrete architecture, and its symbolic flames and geometric maple leaves? Because if this was so, then it had been half a century since I was an adolescent.

Once I recovered from this shock, however, I became intrigued by the idea of writing about objects. Anyone who knows me can attest to the fact that objects have played a significant role in my life (particularly if you believe, as I do, that works of architecture can be classed in the object category). One could say I have spent a lot of time moving in and out of objects, as well as carting a great number of slightly smaller objects in and out of slightly larger objects. Every single one of the objects in question was and remains important to me, not the least because of the captivating stories associated with them. Some of the objects are of ancestral origin, while others were purchased by me in moments of weakness. But each of them possesses a unique narrative, if only concerning the routes they took to become a part of my life.

But as I was to discover, the history of an object itself—the how and why it was fashioned; whether it is organic, or mercantile, or spiritual in nature, or a combination of the three—opens up like a fan to reveal a much, much larger picture. It becomes impossible to think deeply about, for example, a beaver hat without investigating attitudes to animal life, colonization, ecology, the fur trade, capitalism, imperialism, the use and misuse of natural resources, and on and on. The same is true of a pine board, a concrete block, or a gas tank. But sometimes the objects in question are more innocent and uplifting: a dance hall, a revered rock face, a simple pair of spectacles, or a medal given to a Canadian for his contribution to world peace.

One of the big questions that arises from the existence of this book (which is itself an object) is why I was chosen to assemble these objects. The answer can only be connected to serendipity. My fiction has sometimes been associated with Canadian history, and long passages of it are concerned with a closely observed world. But I have not spent my life examining every single object in the part of North America known as Canada. Nor do I consider myself to be in a position to make judgments about what should and shouldn't be included in a list of things Canadian. I was asked, and I said yes, and after I said yes, I began to write about phenomena that interested and moved me. Another author would undoubtedly have picked an entirely different set of objects.

The title occurred to me quite early on. *The world is so full of a number of things*, I thought, remembering the couplet by Robert Louis Stevenson, *I'm sure we should all be as happy as kings*. It wasn't long before I realized that not everything I was writing about was happy in the way that term is most often defined. (Also, to be honest, I am not certain that kings are all that happy.) I liked the poem too much to change it, however, and so, for my own purposes, I opened up the word *happy*. In my life I have been happiest when I have been engaged with or interested in a person, an art form, a narrative, an object, the unfolding of certain events. I decided to allow the word *happy* to include a state of fascination—whether that fascination attached itself to the dark or the light, or to various shades and shadows in between.

The amount I learned about this country, simply by turning my attention to fifty objects one after another, is immeasurable—so much so that I would advise readers of this book to research their own fifty objects to see where that quest might lead them in terms of a greater understanding of Canada. That being said, one of the most exciting things I learned was that Canada is always under revision, and probably will remain a work-in-progress for as long as it exists. Canada has never developed an official history, for instance. Nor has it adopted an official cultural standpoint—or at least not one that stuck. This lack of certainty about identity, once seen as a drawback of being a colony, has allowed for multiple points of view and a greater-than-average amount of adaptability. And it has contributed, in my opinion, to the growth of a nation that is full of a delightful and fascinating number of things, people, cultures, animals, birds, landscapes, arts, books, theatres, sports, politics, religions.

There were surprises as I worked on this book, of course—and plenty of them. One surprise, at least to me, was that while I had believed that Canada—especially now—was essentially a secular country, it in fact concerns itself with things of a spiritual nature, in some form or another, on a daily basis. First Nations tribes still focus on the preservation of nature, and know that it is important to show respect for the spirits of the land and the elements. While some of the lovely English-style churches that I connect with my childhood have sagging roofs and dwindling congregations, new examples of religious architecture are appearing in our landscape, thanks to both the reverence and the vitality of some of our more recent immigrants, whose systems of belief are both ancient and permanent. In a less formal way, many of us look quietly inside ourselves for guiding principles, or find ourselves defining quality of life in a way that is not necessarily rooted in enterprise or gain.

There were also large and startling contradictions that revealed themselves as I looked into the history of these objects—undeniable injustices on the one hand, and the existence of the Canadian Charter of Rights and Freedoms on the other. Or careless and greedy harvesting of natural resources set against the Canadian people's love of and respect for wilderness landscapes.

A large portion of this book was created not by me but by the gifted draughtsman and illustrator Scott McKowen. Early in the process I asked Scott if he would consider drawing the objects I had selected, and not only did he agree, but he entered into the project with a more than generous amount of enthusiasm. Much better organized than I, Scott not only kept a master list of the objects he was drawing, but also made some important suggestions, the Five Roses sign and the votive ship among them. His wife and creative partner, Christina Poddubiuk, introduced the notion of the codfish as the best object from Newfoundland. She also provided the belt for the illustration of the schoolbooks and made clarifying observations concerning some of the other objects on the list.

This is a magnificent country in which to live, for all kinds of reasons. Yes, there are flaws in the system, inequalities and injustices. But we have the tools to address these problems, and an openness to the idea of attempting to change for the better. In the end I came to realize how much I love Canada, and how fortunate I am that my ancestors were among the waves of refugees and immigrants who, for several hundred years now, have arrived on its shores. I also came more fully to understand the great debt we settlers—whether multi-generational or brand new—owe to the First Peoples of Canada, whose territories and ways of life were—and continue to be—undeniably altered by our presence.

I confidently expect that we will rewrite and rewrite this country into the foreseeable future. Undoubtedly, there will be many new and better versions of Canada under construction as time goes by. I for one look forward with optimism to exploring the new terrain and to reading the revisions.

A NUMBER OF THINGS

Legging

AS A MOTHER, NOTHING IS MORE TERRIFYING to contemplate, or unthinkably tragic to experience, than the death of your child. But if you are on the cusp of extinction—one of the last mothers of your culture, burying one of the last children—this appalling sorrow expands to even greater proportions.

The Beothuk were a hunter-gatherer indigenous people who, until the nineteenth century, inhabited the large island known to European migratory fishermen, and eventually to settlers, as Newfoundland. Since 1949, Newfoundland and its mainland neighbour, Labrador, have been Canada's newest, as well as its most easterly, province. But by the time the province's soon-to-be first premier, Joey Smallwood, was encouraging the British colony to vote in favour of joining Canada, not a trace of the Beothuk had been seen for well over a hundred years.

Several theories—all involving Western contact—have been brought forward to explain the extinction. They range from conscious genocide perpetrated by white settlers, to starvation brought on by lack of access to traditional Beothuk hunting and fishing grounds increasingly occupied by these same settlers, to a less violent (but no less deadly) spread of European infectious diseases. Various narratives about "the Last Beothuk" have swirled around the subject as well—the most poignant being the story of Shanawdithit, who was captured by the British in 1823, and who, before she died of consumption in 1829, passed on to us through drawings and oral history the little that we know of her people. Her skull, which ended up—for study purposes—in the Royal College of Physicians in London, England, was destroyed, along with the building that housed it, during the Second World War.

To see one's people disappear is to have the very meaning of human existence torn apart in one's lifetime. And yet, it seems that love itself still exists, even when the world and everyone in it are shattered and on the verge of extinction. This artefact, taken from a Beothuk child's burial site discovered in 1827 and currently in the collection of the Rooms museum in St. John's, speaks eloquently about that love. There would have been too few tribesmen still alive to make the traditional box-and-skin body bag for the burial of this anonymous Beothuk child. More than likely in a starving condition herself, the mother would have had nothing to work with but her ochre-painted leggings made of beaver hide and decorated with bird claws and bone pendants. It is to be hoped that as she removed that legging from her left leg and wrapped it around her dead child's body, she believed the infant would be warmed on his or her journey to the spirit world.

Skull

THE WAY THAT WE KEEP OUR DEAD IN OUR collective imagination—how we transform them into ghosts, angels, or saints—is a significant marker in the various cultures that have flourished or faded in the vast geography we now call Canada. Catholicism, with its statues, paintings, religious architecture, elaborate marble tombs, and reliquaries displaying the bones of saints, was a strong presence in the New World for the first couple of centuries after Western settlement. This was particularly true in the French colony of Quebec, where the first religious order, the Recollects, arrived as early as 1615. They were followed by the Jesuits in 1625, and after some coaxing, Ursuline nuns from Tours and Bordeaux in 1639. The latter had to spend their first winters in an empty fur warehouse in the makeshift, roughshod harbour of Quebec before finally gaining entrance to their newly built convent in 1642.

It was into the chapel of this convent (by means of an opening in the foundation created by enemy cannon fire) that the dying Marquis Louis-Joseph de Montcalm was brought on September 13, 1759, after incurring fatal wounds during the Battle of the Plains of Abraham. The battle, which was part of the Seven Years' War, was ultimately and significantly won by the British. Quebec was surrendered to the English, and the notion of New France becoming a purely British colony was moved to the fore.

The British commander, General James Wolfe, was also killed during the battle, and this fact forever linked the names of Wolfe and Montcalm in the Canadian imagination, even though the two men never met. Various romantic death scenes were painted—particularly of Wolfe's demise—the most famous being Benjamin West's 1770 rendition of the event, which is said to be the first neoclassical painting to depict contemporary, rather than classical, battle garb. François-Louis-Joseph Watteau's 1783 brush drawing, *The Death of Montcalm*, also uses the uniforms of the day. But when it came to setting, the French artist seemingly could not bring himself to leave out the standard Middle Eastern tent and palm tree, and these anomalies make the composition more than a little geographically confusing.

Geographical confusion was also the order of the day when it came to memorializing poor General Wolfe, who has monuments in a number of locations. His statue in

Westminster Abbey is draped in a bronze mantle that includes a rendering of him leading his troops up a geographically unconvincing cliff toward the Plains of Abraham. He can also be seen atop the doorway of the Quebec National Assembly in the company of his French foe, the marquis, both commanders waving cheerfully to passersby. On the Plains of Abraham itself, there is a memorial column purportedly marking the place where Wolfe fell. His remains, however, crossed the ocean and were buried beneath the stone flags of St Alfege Church in his hometown of Greenwich.

I can recall that as schoolchildren, we were often encouraged to sing "The Maple Leaf Forever," the old imperialist song that began with this verse:

In Days of yore
From Britain's shore
Wolfe the dauntless hero came
And planted firm Britannia's flag
On Canada's fair domain.

Montcalm also achieved celebrity status in the classroom, especially with those of us who liked to read, by acting as a character in James Fenimore Cooper's novel *The Last of the Mohicans.*

Unlike those of General Wolfe, however, the remains of Montcalm did not return to the Old World, and were instead interred beneath the floor of the chapel into which he had been brought the night before he died. Sometime later the notion of exposing his relics must have occurred to the good Ursuline sisters, as reference to the skull in the reliquary can be found in more than one nineteenth-century travel guide. (Details of how the skull came to be separated from the rest of the skeleton remain unclear.) I myself saw the skull in the Ursuline convent in the 1990s. Since 2002, however, the marquis—skull and all—has been reunited with many of his troops, who were buried after the battle in the graveyard of the Hôpital-Général of Quebec City.

Hat

L IKE GENERAL WOLFE BEFORE HIM, MAJOR General Isaac Brock sustained fatal wounds in the battle that made him famous. There was a river entailed in his demise as well (the Niagara, not the St. Lawrence), and an elevated terrain above that river (Queenston Heights, not the Plains of Abraham). But unlike the Quebec conflict half a century before, Brock's skirmish did not involve the French. By 1812, there was a foe nearer to hand: the Americans, who, since their own revolution, had had their eyes on the northern part of the continent, which was still under British control. The War of 1812 looked as if it might provide the opportunity to defeat the British and seize the prize.

This war was a complicated affair, fought by the Americans against the British in several different theatres and for a number of different reasons. Although it was viewed in Europe as a subplot to the ongoing Napoleonic Wars, there was plenty of action in North America: blockades off the New England coast, skirmishes as far south as New Orleans, and lots of cannon fire on the Great Lakes in the north. On October 13, 1812—having been defeated at Fort Detroit a few months earlier by Brock and his ally, the Shawnee chief Tecumseh (who was hoping to protect his people from further American expansion in the west)—the Americans crossed the Niagara River at Lewiston and attacked Queenston. Brock, awakened in the night by gunfire, hastily assembled his troops and rode with them up the cliff, thereby becoming an easy target. He was fatally wounded by a sniper's bullet as he attempted to rally his men. Versions of his last words abound. Some would have us believe he shouted, "Push on, brave York Volunteers!" as he fell from his horse. Others insist he said, "Push on, don't mind me," or simply the Latin word "*Surgite!*" But in the end, most historians have agreed that Brock was killed instantly and wouldn't have had time to say anything at all, in spite of the significant fact that what he and his troops accomplished means that we are still Canadian to this day.

The other thing he would not have had time to do was don this handsome hat. At the moment of Brock's death, the hat, housed in its shiny, black tricorne tin box, was still in the hold of a ship that was making its way across the Atlantic. Nevertheless, in most period renderings of his death, Brock's hat is present, its splendid red ostrich plume rising like a

fountain of blood above the coffin-like rectangle of the black structure beneath.

The hat *did* arrive in time for a couple of his funerals, however, and was proudly displayed at the last two of them. Brock was first buried—a few days after his death—in the northwest corner of Fort George at Niagara-on-the-Lake. In 1840, his remains were disinterred and reburied on the battlefield of Queenston Heights, at the site of the large column erected as a monument in his name. Twelve years later, after an Irish rebel blew up this monument, Brock was finally, and irrevocably, buried inside the limestone column—still in good repair today in spite of a 1929 lightning strike—that replaced the first.

As for the hat, it had been passed around and posed under by a century of local militiamen—and was somewhat frayed and soiled as a result—when it found a permanent home in the Niagara Historical Society and Museum. There it sits, looking almost alive with its tufts of plumage and its circular knot of black ribbons known as a cockade. It is so animal-like that an aura of faithfulness seems to surround it. One cannot help thinking it might have taken the bullet for Brock, had it only arrived in time.

Ship

A FOREST OF MASTS IN A HARBOUR, THE unfurling of unthinkably large canvas sails into the Atlantic or Pacific wind, views of coastlines approaching or receding, terror in the face of storm—very little of this is now a part of human travel. But without ships, and without the cargo they brought to and from the New World, Canada would not be the country it is today. And without the men who learned the skills associated with a life on the high seas, these ships could not have sailed.

Sailors were considered to be mere mortals when they were plentiful upon the earth. But from this distance they seem to have been like a pantheon of gods who, under extreme and ever-changing conditions, managed the empires of cloth and arteries of rope that made up the world of the ship. The athletic choreography on the deck and among the masts of a sailing ship was played out to appeals and commands

shouted in Shakespearean language from one rope ladder to another. The whole performance must have been a wonder to behold.

Notre-Dame-de-Bon-Secours Chapel in Montreal is sometimes called the Sailors' Church. Its proximity to the port and the presence on its roof of a statue of the Virgin as the Star of the Sea may constitute two of the reasons for this. Most magical, however, are the ship models, or votive ships, that hang from the ceiling of this place of worship. They were made by sailors as offerings to the Virgin, to whom they had prayed during times of peril. Essentially, therefore, these miniature vessels are requited prayers made tangible, and as such are beautiful and moving works of art. They could only have been made by someone who had danced all over a ship—someone who knew every inch of its decks and sails and rigging, from the mainsail right down to its last small, brightly coloured scrap of a signal flag. To imagine these vital, physical men sitting down to such a quiet and delicate task makes us feel as though we have shared an intimate moment with them, during which they confessed to us their love of the ship for which they had prayed, and their love of the life they were given.

Black Rock

ROOTED DEEP IN THE LEGENDS RECOUNTED by my mother's large tribal family, the Quinns, is the story of the letter from Ireland. According to my mother, who insisted she once saw it as a child, the letter was written in the latter half of the nineteenth century by members of the family still living in the "old" country to those who, for a dozen years or so, had been situated in the new. It was received deep in the Canadian backwoods, and addressed the fact that in the New World the family had decided to become Protestant, or "go Proddy," as vernacular speech would have it. My mother was vague about who in the family had written the letter from Ireland, and to whom it had been addressed, but her memory concerning the sentiments expressed therein was crystal clear. The Irish members of the family had forever severed relations with their Canadian cousins, who, in their opinion, had betrayed

them in the most heinous possible way. They had given up the Catholic religion.

There would have been good reasons for this seemingly radical decision taken by my Canadian ancestors. (If indeed they did take it—there is also a version of this story suggesting that they had already given up Catholicism before they left Ireland, and that this perceived defection may have explained their need to depart.) It was not easy to be an Irish Catholic in Protestant Orange Order–dominated Upper Canada. At the worst of times one's barns might be burned, and at the best of times one would be subjected to a quiet but pervasive discrimination. Once the Quinns became Protestants, they would have had a much better shot at "getting ahead," which they, like most immigrants, had at least partly in mind when they came to this new land. Or if, as some suggest, they were already Protestant when they left Ireland, they would have had a much better chance of surviving the journey, as the ship on which they travelled would have been in superior condition to those used by British landlords to transport their often ill and mostly Catholic tenants to the New World.

Protestant or Catholic, they were fortunate in one respect: they sailed in 1842, a good half decade before the year that would be forever known as Black 47.

By 1847, the infamous potato blight had destroyed several harvests in Ireland, and the famine, which had always been a threat in that country, was at its peak. Literally hundreds of thousands of people were dying of starvation and associated contagions. It is estimated that between 1845 and 1850, close to one million people, out of a population of eight million, died. A further two million people sought refuge in other parts of the world—in Australia, the United States, and the territory then known as British North America. Quite a number died en route of "ship fever" in what came to be known as the "coffin ships." It is said that between June and August of 1847, there were so many weak and starving Irish immigrants arriving in the St. Lawrence River that the line of these ships stretched, bow to stern, for a dozen miles downstream from the quarantine station at Grosse-Île. Many of those who survived the ocean voyage contracted typhus either in this dark traffic jam or while later being processed at Grosse-Île, and those who did not die while in quarantine often fell ill once they reached the docks at Quebec City and Montreal. Those who endured fanned out over Upper and Lower Canada.

Between 1830 and 1850, over five hundred thousand Irish immigrants—my ancestors included—were introduced to Canada in this manner. In 1847, however, the number of immigrants was so high and the situation so dire that fever sheds were built at Windmill Point in Montreal to alleviate the overcrowding on Grosse-Île, and even though the area was fenced off so that the Irish could not escape, the contagion swept like an unstoppable nightmare into the city. Grey nuns, priests, and the mayor of Montreal himself all died while attending the sick. In the end, six thousand Irish immigrants died in these sheds over the period of one year. It is worth pointing out that over a thousand Irish orphans were adopted by French-speaking Catholics in Montreal and Quebec City.

A decade later, while they were sinking a pylon in the construction of the Victoria Bridge, Irish labourers came across a huge mass grave. Some of these labourers might have known—or would have been related to—the victims they had mistakenly unearthed, and the accompanying horror and sorrow would have been simply unimaginable. An oversized black rock in the vicinity was used to create a memorial on which the following words were carved:

TO

PRESERVE FROM DESECRATION

THE REMAINS OF 6000 IMMIGRANTS

WHO DIED OF SHIP FEVER

A.D. 1847–8.

THIS STONE

IS ERECTED BY THE WORKMEN

OF

MESS[RS] PETO, BRASSEY & BETTS.

EMPLOYED IN THE CONSTRUCTION

OF THE

VICTORIA BRIDGE

A.D. 1859

The rock now sits on a median that itself is like a quarantine island between two flowing streams of traffic. The Irish, and subsequently Italian, immigrant neighbourhoods that surrounded it have been razed and replaced by what seem to be semi-vacant parking lots. This is not an easy monument to visit—not physically, and not emotionally. It remains in place, obdurate but mostly ignored in the midst of freeways, billboards, and hydro towers. And still, once a year, a group of Irish or Canadians of Irish descent walk to "the Stone," to remember the six thousand sons and daughters of Ireland who died in Montreal.

Cowcatcher

LADY SUSAN AGNES MACDONALD, SECOND WIFE of our much-praised and frequently criticized first prime minister, turns out to have been an unusual woman, especially if one considers the times, and the places, that influenced her life. Daughter of a Jamaican plantation owner, she would have witnessed not only the daily brutality and moral corruption of owning slaves, but also some of Jamaica's most bloody and ultimately successful uprisings. For obvious reasons, her father's fortunes did not fare well in Jamaica after the 1838 emancipation of the slaves, and when he died in 1850, the family moved to Ontario, where Hewitt, one of her two brothers, became secretary to a man called John A. Macdonald, the attorney general of Canada West (as it was named at the time).

Living in Ontario did not prevent Agnes from making frequent trips to the mother country, and thus it was that in 1866 she happened to be in England for the London Conference, during which the British North America Act was hammered out in preparation for Canadian Confederation. John A., allegedly a great wit, announced that he had become so fond of the notion of unity he felt he should try it out once again himself, and the two were married and even managed a short honeymoon in Oxford while the conference grumbled on around them. The BNA Act was duly drafted and signed, and when the Dominion of Canada was born on July 1, 1867, John A. became Sir John A. and his wife became Lady Macdonald.

Years later, in 1886, as first lady to the first prime minister, Agnes would accompany her husband on his only journey to the West Coast—one that would be taken on the almost new transcontinental train, the last spike having been driven into the earth of British Columbia in 1885. Sir John was in his second incarnation at the time: the Pacific Scandal, in which the construction of the railway was politically encouraged by massive campaign donations from promoters of same, had thrown him out of office for a while in the 1870s. His problems with alcohol had not abated to any noticeable degree, and if there was a bar car, he was likely spending a considerable amount of time in it.

Travel in previous centuries astonishes, especially if one considers the amount of time spent moving over land or across oceans without showers or sleeping pills. This, added to the very real dangers along the route (weather, mechanical

failure, accidents, disease), arguably made *any* travel extreme travel. In spite of this, Lady Agnes apparently wanted adventures even more thrilling than those already provided, and when the train eventually reached the Rocky Mountains, she announced to a thunderstruck superintendent that she would be travelling on the engine's cowcatcher for the final six hundred miles of the journey to avail herself of a better view. She was able to persuade her husband to join her for only thirty miles, but from the sounds of her diary, his absence in no way diminished her enjoyment. Perhaps her enthusiasm encouraged her husband to think seriously about preserving such extraordinarily beautiful landscapes, as shortly after the couple returned from the west, Sir John established Yoho and Glacier national parks, two of our first mountain parks.

Lady Agnes never forgot the mountains. And the mountains would remember her as well. There is a small body of water near the top of Mount St. Piran called Lake Agnes, and Mount Lady Macdonald looms over Canmore. And her excitement en route is touchingly expressed in *By Car and Cowcatcher*, her published account of the experience. Reading it, one feels one is sitting right beside her on the biscuit box that the engineer had affixed to the triangular iron platform as a provisional chair. "There is glory of brightness and beauty everywhere," she enthuses, "and I laugh aloud on the cowcatcher, just because it is all so delightful."

Sampler

EASY TO PICK UP AND PUT DOWN IN MOMENTS stolen from the chores of the day, the sampler, a piece of cloth through which one could draw coloured threads, came naturally to the female hand. The art of decorative stitchery, therefore, has almost always been the domain of girls and women. First Nations women, for example, have proven to be exceptionally skilful and inventive with a needle, whether they are using leather lacing or beads and embroidery thread. In the convents of seventeenth-century Quebec, Ursuline nuns of earliest New France made vivid *tapisseries* based on similar works in Europe. A short while later, in the kitchens and parlours of eighteenth- and nineteenth-century Upper and Lower Canada, girls as young as eight employed the cross-stitch method to depict numbers and the alphabet in their samplers, which, as the name suggests, were a means of practising various stitches. Sometimes, however, these girls

branched out, rendering animals and birds, and creating frontal views of houses.

I can recall some of the late-eighteenth- and nineteenth-century samplers that my mother, a dedicated collector of antiques, hung on the walls of our house. Small, faded, and filled with numerals and upper- and lowercase letters, they sometimes included grim little verses, the rendering of which, I suspect, was meant to keep these girl children in line. One read thus:

> *The rose is fragrant but it fades in time*
> *The violet sweet but quickly past the prime*
> *White lilies hang their heads and soon decay*
> *And white snow in minutes melts away*
> *Such and so withering are our early joys*
> *Which time and sickness speedily destroys.*

The creator of that particular sampler, Sarah Miller, who added her name and age at the bottom of her work, was nine years old.

Catherine Clarke, who, in 1858, lived in the now practically non-existent settlement of Bathurst, in eastern Ontario, does not state her age on the sampler illustrated here, but her skill with a needle suggests that she must have been a bit older than nine. Unlike Sarah Miller, she does not include a grim little verse in her composition, but instead celebrates the perceived world by portraying birds, flowers, and two abundant and exotic-looking fruit trees. Gone is the alphabet, and in its place stands a handsome house fronted by an enclosed formal garden.

It is very unlikely that anyone living in Bathurst, Upper Canada, in 1858 would have ever seen a house as grand as the one Catherine chose for the subject of her sampler. But the choice itself suggests that, at least at this time of her life, Catherine Clarke had hopes that her domestic future might include something as prosperous, orderly, and attractive as the house she was so painstakingly stitching. Sadly, this was not to be the case, and tales handed down by Catherine's descendants paint a very different picture. Catherine married at a young age, having fallen in love with a man who would ultimately leave her alone in pioneer rural Canada with two small children. She was forced to take in laundry, or to work as hired help in various neighbouring farm kitchens. She died in young middle age—some say by her own hand.

But one of her children saved this sampler and passed it down to one of her own children, and so on from generation to generation. The second-to-last owner, Catherine's great-granddaughter, had it beautifully framed before she brought it into her own home in Huron County, Ontario, where her oldest daughter, Catherine's great-great-granddaughter, admired it while she was a schoolgirl and then took it into her own home once she was grown.

Catherine's great-great-granddaughter still looks at this sampler every day, and thinks about the hard life that awaited its creator. Like her mother, she has lived for most of her life in Huron County. Her name is Alice Munro, and she has spent her adult life writing multi-faceted short stories concerning the mostly rural lives of girls and women. In 2013, she became the first Canadian to win the Nobel Prize in Literature.

Books

I N 1884, WHEN THE MINISTRY OF EDUCATION FOR the province of Ontario decided to create a set of Ontario Readers rather than use, as it had until that moment, the thirty-one titles the British had created for the Irish National Schools series of schoolbooks, it was opening up a venture that would manifest all the good, bad, and ugly features that have attached themselves to the Canadian book world ever since. Companies, of course, fought for the privilege of being the printer/publisher for such a guaranteed market, with W.J. Gage and Company of Toronto emerging temporarily victorious. But arguments were also fought over price, paper quality, and content, as well as, and perhaps more important, what the books were meant to accomplish, beyond the acquisition of the skill of reading. Loyalty to empire, moral instruction, and even some (though admittedly not much) Canadian content came into play.

I own an 1884 edition of the *Second Reader*. My maternal grandmother's name, Fleda Andrus, is written on the flyleaf, though there are names of earlier owners alongside hers. This suggests that the price—twenty cents—would have been too steep for a pioneer household such as hers, and the book was bought second-hand. I also have an *Ontario Readers Third Book*, which I picked up at a yard sale some years ago. By its publication in 1909, the price was only fourteen cents and the Canadian content had become more plentiful and more self-conscious. The book had progressed beyond mere descriptions of the Black Bear, White Bear, and Chipmonk [*sic*], and now included poetry—such as "A Canadian Camping Song" by Sir James David Edgar, and "Jacques Cartier" by Thomas D'Arcy McGee. There were also, sprinkled throughout the text, blurry black-and-white photographs depicting noteworthy Canadian scenery. The only colour image was of the Union Jack, under which, printed in bold, were the words "One Flag, One Fleet, One Throne."

In spite of the admirable attempt to give a nod to Canada, the Ontario Readers had not changed that much in the two decades since they were introduced. Beyond the poem by the former (and now dead) member of Parliament McGee and the poem by the former (and now dead) member of Parliament and Speaker of the House of Commons Edgar (did only politicians write poetry in those days?), as well as a short history of the Battle of Queenston Heights, all topics and authors were imported from England. Subject matter either concerned nature, as would be expected at the tail end of the Romantic period, or described battle. There is a surprising amount of gore, and children seem to be often sacrificed, or to sacrifice themselves, for various noble reasons. "The minstrel boy to the war is gone / In the ranks of death you'll find him" and "The boy stood on the burning deck" pretty much set the tone. But the one thing that must have both confused and fascinated the landlocked children of nineteenth-century Ontario was the sheer number of maritime disasters poetically presented in these readers. Shipwrecks abound and drowning seems to be the only proper way to die. Almost everyone goes down with a smile, or else, as in the case of "The Wreck of the *Orpheus*," the whole company cheers!

Still, these are wonderful poems written by some of the greats, and the very unfamiliarity of the terrain in which the stories they tell unfold must have made them even more thrilling. Furthermore, the fact that over a hundred years ago, children were reading the Ontario Readers and memorizing the poetry in them may very well have played a part in creating the strong relationship Canadians have had with books ever since. My grandmother, for example, had read every book in the small Castleton library twice by the time she was fourteen, and she went on to be an avid reader for the rest of her long life, as did my mother in her wake.

Canadians love their libraries and their small bookstores, and in spite of all efforts to discourage us, we are very loyal to our own authors, whether they write about camping in the Canadian wilds or never make reference to a Canadian landscape at all.

Tractor

WHEN MY UNCLE CLIFF QUINN WAS IN HIS eighties, he decided to write a memoir concerning the family farm on which he had lived for most of his life. Although his formal education ended not long after grade school, Cliff possessed a lively intelligence, a deep love of reading, and an alert curiosity that increased rather than waned as the years went by. He was interested in almost everything: animals, birds, travelling circuses, windmills, the Klondike, stumping machines, barns, the United Farmers of Ontario, village fairs, brook trout, threshing machines, blacksmiths, peddlers, axes, and bees. And he wrote about such things in his memoir. But the two longest chapters were reserved for the two subjects that he cared about most: workhorses and tractors.

To Cliff's mind, the latter were a sort of mechanized version of the former and could both possess a nature and

take on various moods. As a consequence, Cliff himself could and did develop relationships with his tractors, and was much fonder of some than he was of others (though it should be said here that he was *always* fond of the horses, which were more like members of the family). In the mid-1930s, the Quinns (my grandfather and my uncles) began to borrow a neighbour's Rumely Oil Pull tractor, and after its first performance, it was treated with the wonder and respect it deserved. But it did not belong to them, and the relationship, therefore, never really took. Then, in the late 1930s, my grandfather purchased a temperamental Fordson tractor with a bad ignition history, which caused tension on chilly mornings. (Cliff's brother, my uncle Don, often lit fires under the machine on cool mornings, saying he didn't really care if the tractor started or burned up.) Finally, around 1940, the Fordson was traded in for a beautiful new Massey-Harris tractor, which, as Cliff writes, was the first rubber-tired tractor in Cramahe Township. It could pull three ploughs and could manage an acre every hour. Everyone on the farm loved this tractor, which, beyond the field, proved itself useful in many different ways: grading roads, operating as a snowplough on farm lanes, and acting as a suitable subject for a good deal of boasting.

About the same time as my uncles and my grandfather were enjoying their acre an hour, B.K. Sandwell, the then editor of *Saturday Night* magazine, famously quipped,

"Toronto has no social classes / Only the Masseys and the masses," for the Masseys had become enormously rich selling farm machinery. So had the Harrises, with whom, after decades of fierce competition, the Masseys merged in 1891. Once they had merged, thereby doubling their size, they did what most good giant corporations do and began to devour everything in sight. Verity Plow, Bain Wagon, Kemp Manure Spreader, and Johnston Harvester were all under their roof by 1910. By 1919, after distributing American tractors for several years, they issued the Massey-Harris Number 1 tractor. By the time my grandfather had saved up the astronomical sum of eight hundred dollars—which he needed, along with the old Fordson, to purchase his new rubber-wheeled tractor—he would have been looking at a Number 101 Super or Senior model, of which some thousands were sold that year.

The tractor earned its keep. Cliff recalls that one of the fields on the farm was "loaded with quack grass." He and his brothers used the new Massey-Harris tractor and a spring tooth cultivator to plough the field in the fall. "We really tore it up," he writes. The next year, they planted peas and the result was a bumper crop, worth about seventeen hundred dollars on the market. But not everything was about money. One day shortly after the arrival of the tractor, Cliff ploughed a thirteen-acre field at the speed of one acre an hour, and when he was finished, the sun was going down in the west. "I looked back over that field," he writes, "and all across it you could see spider webs. This was quite amazing to me as I had just ploughed the whole field that day. A testimonial to the spiders' indestructability, I'd say."

This is a glimpse of the closely observed world of a small farmer over half a century ago. What would that son of the Massey-Harris empire, artist Lawren Harris, have made of such a sight? By then he had stopped painting the kind of landscapes that would make him, and other members of the Group of Seven, deservedly famous, and had begun a series of spiritually based abstract works inspired by his fascination with theosophy. Perhaps these miraculous webs, created by diligent spiders in the wake of mechanization, would have somehow connected landscape, spirituality, his family's fortune, and the abstract for him, and he would have smiled.

Ferry

SINCE ITS EARLIEST DAYS ON THE BAY, THIS little watercraft has given rise to extreme dramas. An unlikely proposition to begin with—given the convenience and speed of other kinds of water travel, as opposed to the two muddy arms of the Asa Danforth road (now Highway 33) it was meant to join—the Glenora Ferry has sailed, horse-powered, steamed, and chugged across the Bay of Quinte, toward and away from Stone Mills (later called Glenora), for over two hundred years. In its many floating forms, it has been well maintained, badly neglected, refitted, dry-docked, praised, cursed, temporarily abandoned, argued over, storm-stayed, bought, sold, and sunk. People have thrown up on it and given birth in it, and more than one individual has fallen off it and drowned. Its ferrymen have been factory owners, farmers, crooks, drunks, community leaders, extortionists, and members of Parliament, and have occasionally been all these things at the same time. Lawsuits have been launched in its name, and legendary family feuds—some lasting until the present day—have been engendered on its decks. And all this for passage over less than a mile of open water.

The ferry made its first voyage shortly after the American Revolution, when hundreds of New Englanders loyal to the British Crown began to settle in Upper Canada on a sizable tract of land in what would come to be known as Prince Edward County. Indented with bays and surrounded on three sides by the waters of Lake Ontario, "the County" was almost an island, and the feeling of separation from the mainland is still palpable to the visitor. Back in the late eighteenth century, when Asa Danforth's road arrived in the vicinity, those who had been brave enough to slog along this muddy thoroughfare all the way from York had to find a way to cross the narrows of the bay so that they could continue their progress toward Kingston.

The two rural landscapes joined by the ferry are similar in tone, and neither has changed all that much in the past two centuries. Tidy and bucolic, the fields cleared by settlers remain well fertilized and well fenced, and architecturally significant historic houses are still miraculously intact. The view in either direction, therefore, is much the same today as it has always been, and a mysterious and beautiful geography continues to exist in the vicinity of both harbours. The land rears up abruptly from the ferry dock in Glenora, creating

an escarpment that cries out for a fortress. Instead, two hundred feet above Lake Ontario, the small, wondrous, and (by popular belief) bottomless Lake on the Mountain shines like a silver disc in the otherwise flat pasture of a plateau. On the Adolphustown side, the highway, now named the Loyalist Parkway, moves through stately villages and follows the edge of the lake. Islands named for stern British generals loom offshore and tempt the traveller with their own ferries.

The narrow neck of water in the Bay of Quinte that the Glenora Ferry traverses is called Adolphus Reach. Some of the more operatic members of the communities on both sides were said to be able to call to one another across the reach on calm nineteenth-century days, and I suspect that the ferryman himself might have been one of the callers. That one word, *reach*, suggests that one is leaning toward the far shore, wanting more than a voice, yearning for both union and transformation. The myths, songs, and poems that have always been associated with ferries are brought to mind by the word. As are tales of the handsome boatman who sometimes turns out to be both lover and guide to the otherworld or underworld—that place where the magical scenery is askew and lakes with no known source gleam on the tops of unexpected mountains.

Staffordshire Dogs

BECAUSE THE AMALGAMATION OF SOME OF THE colonies was loosely hammered out at the Charlottetown Conference in 1864, Prince Edward Island, Canada's smallest province both by size and in terms of its population, is known as the Cradle of Confederation. Interestingly, in spite of hosting the Charlottetown talks, the Island itself was very much against signing on, and would not be persuaded to join until six years after official Confederation was enacted in 1867. Islanders are spunky people. Until very recently, they could be heard speaking about Upper Canadians in a dismissive fashion, as a group considerably less sophisticated than themselves—more likely, I suppose, to be "railroaded into something" (if you will forgive the pun). None of this, however, did anything to abate the party atmosphere at the 1864 conference. After each day of talks there was a banquet for the delegates, and then, to wrap it all up, on the last day of the conference, a ball was held to honour the occasion. Amazingly, there was even a visiting circus in town when the delegates arrived in early September.

In 1874, a year after Prince Edward Island succumbed to the lure of Confederation, a girl was born who would put the new province firmly on the map. Granddaughter of Senator Donald Montgomery, one of the first Canadian senators to come from the Island, Lucy Maud Montgomery was born into what was regarded as Island aristocracy, something she would never forget. Her mother died when she was only twenty-one months old, and her father remarried, then settled in Prince Albert, Saskatchewan, leaving his small daughter in the care of her maternal grandparents. Although her grandparents were strict and confining—and as an only child being raised by an elderly couple, she was often lonely—Lucy Maud Montgomery was not fully unhappy. She loved the rural landscape of Prince Edward Island, and when visiting Park Corner, the home of her senator grandfather, she was able to happily interact and play with her cousins in a setting that would serve her well in the future.

She began writing poetry and keeping a diary (a practice she would continue for the rest of her life) at a very early age. From the first page of her first diary, the reader suspects the child is writing it because she thinks she will be famous. And famous she became. After her first novel, *Anne of Green Gables*, was published to acclaim and astonishing sales in 1908—it eventually went on to sell over fifty million copies in twenty different languages—Montgomery was well known on the world stage, and so was Prince Edward Island. Further Anne books appeared over the years, as did the Emily series and numerous short stories and poems. Although Montgomery left Prince Edward Island in 1911, never to return, almost all her books are set there. Two china dogs, whom she named Gog and Magog, appear often in her fiction. They were based on two large pieces of Staffordshire pottery that Montgomery owned.

Montgomery's adult personal life was the shadow side of her mostly cheerful fiction. She married a Presbyterian minister, Ewan Macdonald, who had a series of breakdowns due to a condition known at the time as religious melancholia, and she herself suffered from clinical depression. Her son Chester was a chronic failure, and eventually a liar and a swindler. Her American publisher cheated her out of royalties and film revenue. As her husband's condition worsened, he was forced, after several incoherent sermons, to retire from the ministry. All of this caused Montgomery heartbreak and humiliation.

Gog and Magog, objects of great fun in the fiction, ended up accompanying Montgomery's papers to the University of Guelph at the time of the acquisition of her fonds by that institution's archive. When the archivists received the

china dogs, it was obvious they had been smashed to pieces and then glued back together.

Lucy Maud Montgomery never got a chance to glue her own life back together. In spite of the joy her fiction brought to readers all over the world, and the satisfaction she herself experienced in the face of her considerable achievements, she died at the age of sixty-seven, on April 24, 1942, most likely by her own hand. The last sentences in her journals, written on March 23, 1942, read thus:

"I shall be driven to end my own life. Oh God, forgive me. Nobody dreams what my awful position is."

Barn

ACCORDING TO MY UNCLE CLIFF QUINN'S memoir, and to the various stories recounted by my mother and her other brothers, the earliest barns on my maternal family's farm were ill-fated. The first was laboriously moved from one family farm to another: it was pushed on rollers across several fields by my grandfather and four or five of his brothers. "This was a big operation," Cliff writes. "It involved rollers, planks, and capstans." Settling it in place was no easy task either, and in the stories I heard about that process, the number of workhorses used fluctuated between twenty and two hundred, depending on who was telling the tale. It was a prodigious amount of work by any account, with both animals and humans operating at full strength. It was also apparently overseen by a jealous God. "That same night," Cliff writes, "a terrific windstorm came up and flattened the barn." A few years later, when

the family and neighbours began to build another barn, yet another big wind sprang up over the noon dinner, and brought down the beams and rafters that the men had assembled just that morning. Once a barn was finally completed without elemental interference, it was much appreciated by the Quinns. "Someone told me," writes Cliff, "that after they finished building the big barn, Uncle Art Quinn and Big Art Jones had a wrestling match on the roof." A curious kind of celebration, but a celebration nonetheless!

In a country filled with some of the most desperate weather systems in the world, outbuildings to protect crops, catches, equipment, and animals have been vital to everyone's survival. One thinks of the fishing rooms, large sheds that were until recently an integral part of the outports of Newfoundland, or the lovely, tall grain elevators of the Prairies. One thinks of stables and silos, drive sheds and woodsheds, and the humble little milkhouse, so beloved by Cliff that he took it with him when he left the farm.

Agriculture in Canada changed drastically in the years after the Second World War. All but one of my grandfather's brothers, for example, spent their lives on a farm, whereas only two of my mother's six brothers would become farmers. In the next generation, every single one of the children of these two farmers became a professional and left the land. Industrialization, urbanization, education, and in some odd roundabout way, the postwar use of pesticides all led to this transformation. By 2011, the number of farms would be down by 70 percent, and most recently, the number of people who list their primary occupation as farmer has dropped to 2 percent.

This alteration is visible in our landscapes, as well as in our occupations. Factory farms now resemble huge empty parking lots as the old farmhouses disappear one by one. The barns are disappearing as well. We sometimes glimpse one or two of them as we speed by on a busy freeway. Sagging and abandoned, they look as old and out of place as Roman granaries or Tudor byres inexplicably set down among the industrial warehouses that now occupy what once were fields.

Someone I know once rescued a lintel from the top of the two main doors of a stone barn that was about to be torn down in Eramosa Township, Ontario. The surrounding fields were being turned into housing lots, and the name of the whole enterprise was to be, ironically, Stone Barn Estates. The message on the stone lintel was more heartfelt and sincere. On it were carved the following words:

When your barn is well filled
All safe and secure
Be grateful to God
And remember the poor.

Rope

LOUIS RIEL'S PERSONALITY WAS FUELLED BY A kind of glorious fury. Propelled by anger concerning the treatment of the Métis in western Canada, he twice participated in armed resistance movements against the Canadian government and its then prime minister, John A. Macdonald. In the end he paid heavily for his principles, was executed as a traitor, and became a legend whose name, and cause, would never be forgotten.

Born in 1844, son of a Métis, or mixed-race, father, Riel was bound by blood and by love of the land to the territory of Rupert's Land (part of which is now the province of Manitoba). Fur was the oil of the times in the mid-nineteenth century, and some of the many French traders and voyageurs who had been associated for the past hundred years with the vast holdings of the Hudson's Bay Company and the North West Company had taken First Nations women for brides.

The children of these unions were called Métis (a variant of the French word for "mixed"), and they came to identify with one another and with the territory they inhabited as a collective cultural unit.

Riel was raised to be a devout Catholic, and while he was enrolled at the Petit Séminaire of Montreal, it looked for a while as if he might actually become a priest. But fate had another profession planned for him—that of passionate political agitator. He left the seminary and returned to his birthplace in the beautiful Red River Valley in order to fight for the rights of the Métis people among whom he was raised. Protestants from Upper Canada, many belonging to the anti-Catholic Orange Order, had increasingly settled in the region, and the British government had plans to transfer Métis lands to the Canadian government. The resulting Red River Rebellion, in which Riel was a key player, and the subsequent establishment of a provisional government would ultimately lead to the founding of the province of Manitoba. But the argument between the Macdonald government and Riel was far from over. Neither Riel nor his cohorts were granted any kind of amnesty, and they fled across the border to Montana, where they remained in exile for several years.

Exile did not agree with Riel: the rebel in him needed a theatre of action. Writing angry poems on the theme of betrayal and dedicating them to Sir John A. Macdonald was, in the end, not enough. Riel knew that even the few promises made to the Métis in the 1870 Manitoba Act were unlikely to be kept. The buffalo, upon which the Métis depended, were gone, and both their home territory and the lands of their full-blood neighbours (Cree, Blackfoot, and Salteaux) were under threat from growing western expansion. In the 1880s, Riel decided to head north to participate in what would come to be known as the North-West Rebellion. Five months after the conflict began, the Canadian military subdued the Métis soldiers, and on July 6, 1885, Riel was charged with treason and eventually sentenced to death. After writing his final poem, he was publicly hanged in Regina on November 16 of the same year.

Souvenirs associated with this tragic parade of events were apparently much sought after at the time. Canadian diplomat Michael Phillips, for instance, recalls that he saw Riel's buckskin coat in the early 1970s in Dublin, Ireland. It had apparently crossed the ocean in the latter part of the nineteenth century among the possessions of a retired soldier who had been involved in Riel's capture. Eventually, the coat found its way into the vaults of the National Museum of Ireland, and it was given to the Canadian embassy in the 1970s. Phillips remembers the artefact being taken back to Canada, carefully packed in a cardboard box.

Pieces of the rope that hanged Riel were also much in demand. As Sandra Martin points out in her September 22, 2012, *Globe and Mail* article on the subject, "nooses were prized as good-luck charms at the time." There are some who say that if one were to braid together all the sections of rope that claim the dubious honour of having silenced forever a voice of such burning intensity, one could encircle (and by extension, hang) the entire province of Manitoba. Still, there are two pieces that rise to the top of the list of most likely suspects: a very frayed collection of strands, now in the Saint-Boniface Museum in Winnipeg but originally in the possession of a former premier of Manitoba, Duff Roblin, and a second in the Royal Canadian Mounted Police Heritage Centre in the city of Regina. The rope itself was the subject of that last poem written by Riel on the eve of his execution:

The rope
Threatens my life; but
Thank God, I fear not.

Shortly before his death, Riel made the following statement:

I am more convinced every day that without a single exception I did right. And I have always believed that, as I have acted honestly, the time will come when the people of Canada will see and acknowledge it.

One hundred and fifty years later, Canadians are finally paying attention to what it was that drove Riel's singular

sense of purpose. In the Daniels decision of April 14, 2016, the Supreme Court ruled that Métis and non-status Indians are "Indians" under s. 91(24) of the Constitution Act, 1867, and that their rights, therefore, should be protected by Ottawa. This officially brings to public attention that Métis and non-status rights were not being upheld, as Riel constantly maintained. But it also begins a long-overdue process of negotiation toward making Métis and non-status lives better.

Louis Riel is buried in the graveyard of Saint-Boniface Cathedral. Saint Boniface is now a city ward of Winnipeg, the capital of Manitoba. He is widely regarded both as a hero and as the founder of that province.

Crosscut Saw

LUMBERJACK IS, UNQUESTIONABLY, A CANADIAN word. Even the British admit this in their *Oxford English Dictionary* definition, where they cite the word's appearance in the 1832 *Cobourg Star*'s letters to the editor as the first instance of the term being used in print. It wouldn't be the last, however; many poems, ballads, tales, novels, and songs were to follow. One thinks immediately of the late great country-and-western singer Stompin' Tom Connors and his famous song "Big Joe Mufferaw," written in 1970, or Monty Python's "Lumberjack Song" of 1969, or the *Lumberjack* movie, released in 1944. Romantic fiction also features lumberjacks among its rugged male characters in books with titles such as *Lumberjack in Love* or the more daring *Lumberjack Werebear*.

These men, who lived in bush shanties and bunk-houses, and who worked outdoors in frigid and dangerous conditions, were much idealized over the years, along with their profession. But the truth was often more prosaic and much more grim. Working in the bush was a necessity for many in early Canada, not a vocation, and it was often the only employment that stood between a man and destitution. Young men regularly left their family kitchens to fell trees in the deep woods, and it was not uncommon for the winter timbering of a back woodlot to bring more money into a farmer's bank account than his fall harvest.

Before the two-man crosscut saw, which came into common use in about 1870, an unimaginable amount of labour went into the felling of the great old-growth forests of the St. Lawrence Valley and Great Lakes region. First, the giant trees were brought to the ground by use of a hand-held timber axe, then branches were removed and the trunk squared and sawed into "stick lengths." Rough trails were cut through the underbrush toward the nearest riverbank or lake edge, where the logs were launched and placed under the care of the river drivers, young men hired for the very dangerous job of riding the timber and breaking up logjams. My great-grandfather was, on occasion, one of these young men.

The eventual destination for the logs was the St. Lawrence River and the docks at Quebec City, where they would be loaded onto ships bound for Europe in general but most often England. These same ships would have recently disgorged hundreds of immigrants, many of whom—if healthy—would

themselves be employed in the timber trade before too many years had passed. A good percentage of the immigrants were Irish, and came from a land where the oaks and the ash had disappeared under a similar kind of removal hundreds of years before.

This system of bringing the immigrants in and the timber out persisted for many years. Between 1840 and 1860, some six hundred thousand loads of timber a year were brought into British ports as Canadian wood went into the making of everything one can imagine, from toothpicks and matches seen in every household to the mainmasts and spars of the British navy. To many, this seemed a very good thing: young men were employed, land was cleared for farming, and the economy on both sides of the Atlantic prospered. It is only recently that this extensive clearance has been seen as the great ecological misfortune that it was. Not one of us will ever see the canopy of a central Canadian old-growth forest, or glimpse any of the several species that were rendered extinct as a result of its disappearance.

As for the first use of the term *lumberjack* in the 1832 *Cobourg Star*, that letter to the editor was—bizarrely—written from the point of view of a wooden bridge that had been damaged by a runaway raft of timber while the minders were enjoying themselves in a nearby tavern. The bridge was highly offended by the negligence of these "lumberjacks," whom it referred to as "an incorrigible, though perhaps useful, race of mortals," and who, according the bridge, were "votaries of Bacchus" and inclined "to spend the night in the worship of the jolly god." Had this taken place a few years later, and given that his home farm was situated just north of Rice Lake, my great-grandfather might have been among them.

Shoe

THE GIGANTIC DOUGLAS FIRS OF VANCOUVER Island once overlooked the back fences of the tidy nineteenth-century residential districts of Victoria, British Columbia. Though there are still vestiges of that combination of picket and totem present in the city's extensive parklands, the shadow thrown on the doorstep by the old-growth forests is now a thing of the past. In the 1870s, however, during the childhood of the seminal artist Emily Carr—a childhood that was lived in the midst of a mannered and strict English-style household—the wild still loomed at the edges.

Her father had done his best to make it disappear, however. As Carr herself tells us in her memoir, *The Book of Small*:

Father wanted his place to look exactly like England.
He planted cowslips and prim-roses and hawthorn

hedges and all the Englishy flowers. He had stiles and
meadows and took away all the wild Canadian-ness
and made it as meek and English as he could.

She was describing one of the family's Sunday walks around the land that her father had bought and tamed on the edge of Beacon Hill Park, the only forest-free part of the landscape surrounding Victoria.

The park itself had a history of gentrification. After James Douglas, the chief factor of the Hudson's Bay Company, had "bought" the Victoria region from First Nations tribes for 371 blankets and a cap (the Hudson's Bay Company already had control of Vancouver Island generally), and after he had encouraged the seven hundred Lekwungen people cultivating the sloping grassy area called Meeacan to move elsewhere, the English set to work planning the band-shells, cricket pitches, and artificial lakes and ponds of a good British park. Like Emily Carr's father, Douglas was as enchanted by the openness of the wildflower-filled grass-land, which he compared to an English meadow, as he was put off by the giant, dark, difficult-to-harvest forests. In most of the park's acreage, however, the wildflowers and grasses were almost immediately chomped down by the herds of farm animals established on the premises to feed the British troops of nearby Fort Victoria.

Perhaps as a result of her father's disdain for the wild,

Emily Carr's psyche, and her art, would bounce back and forth between nature and culture for the first part of her adult life. After studying in San Francisco at the California School of Design in her early youth, she travelled to Europe to receive the academic art training of the time—once to London in 1899, and once to Paris in 1910. Her interest in the aboriginal peoples of British Columbia was always present, however, and after returning from France in 1912, she set out to visit the Queen Charlotte Islands in order to make a record of West Coast totem poles while at least some of them were still standing in the villages where they had been carved. Under the influence of the strong spirituality and unforgettable First Nations sculptural images that she found there, her own brilliant art burst into full flower.

This single piece of leather footwear, which is on loan to the Emily Carr House on Government Street in Victoria, was found in the boarding house that Carr once operated during hard financial times. The subsequent owners, the Porters, and their close friend Jerry Gosley came across the shoe while in the attic of the building looking at paintings Carr had made on the ceiling. Gosley was also a friend of the Victoria-based artist Pat Martin Bates, and when he brought the shoe to her attention, she did a delightful series of prints—now hanging in the University of Victoria's Farquhar Auditorium—called *Emily Carr: A Steppin' Footed Lady*.

This one "shoe" is a fascinating artefact, in that it is clearly a Victorian high-button boot that has been cut down to below the ankle to make it more like a man's shoe. It may have been altered for reasons of comfort—in order to facilitate rough walks in the forests of the Queen Charlotte Islands, for example, or to encourage circulation when standing for long periods of time looking up at trees and totem poles. It could also be seen as an act of defiance, a rebellion against the corseted world of very Victorian Victoria, British Columbia. In her memoir, Emily tells us that even as a child, she wished her family's walks had been "less fenced." In a sense, this boot is a metaphor for everything that became unfenced and unlaced in Emily Carr—how she eventually opened her own eyes and her own heart, and through her art our eyes and our hearts, to the magnificent indigenous culture that fully surrounded and greatly predated the place where she lived.

Grave

THE CANADIAN ARCTIC IS IN MANY WAYS A perfect metaphor for the collective higher consciousness of the nation: uncluttered, vast, and untameable. Furthermore, like our relationship with our own consciousness, our feelings for this most northern part of the country are filled with psychological contradictions. We fight for the sovereignty of our Arctic waters on the one hand, but on the other do very little to combat the poverty and hopelessness that is sometimes part of the lives of Inuit people. We exploit the natural resources of the Far North, but pay next to no attention to the spirituality that the very idea of such a landscape inspires. And now that so many of us live in urban centres, sometimes—I'm tempted to say often—we forget about the Arctic altogether.

Not so the Victorian English. Since the sixteenth century, British explorers and adventurers had been obsessively trying to penetrate the northern polar ice cap in a frenzy that was met with cool indifference by the landscape itself. By the nineteenth century, the Arctic had become an imperial obsession as explorers who set out in ships with names such as the *Terror*, the *Fury*, or the *Griper* (the modern-day equivalent would be the *Schizoid*, the *Psychotic*, or the *Neurotic*) were either frozen in or frozen out, in what appeared to be a difficult and time-consuming variety of male suicide. They were apparently trying to reach the Spice Islands, but surely tasty meals couldn't have been worth all that.

Tasty meals, in fact, may have been the cause of the death of the poor fellows who lie beneath three grave markers on Beechey Island. Members of the most famous and most mysterious expedition of them all—that of John Franklin—they died relatively early in the venture, in 1846, of lead poisoning possibly caused by the enormous store of lead-soldered tinned goods that Franklin had brought with him for the journey. (He'd also packed up a library of three thousand volumes, monogrammed silver cutlery, and a not insignificant number of bottles of wine and spirits.) Another theory suggests that the ships' new desalination equipment, which was installed to turn salt water into fresh, and which contained lead working parts, may have been the culprit.

When Franklin hadn't returned by 1848, the obsession with finding the Northwest Passage evolved into an obsession with finding Franklin, his men, and his ships. Several rescue

expeditions were dispatched and funded by the Crown, and later by Lady Franklin, who came to be an excellent fund-raiser. These new polar seekers and adventurers mapped shorelines and named more than a few islands and straits after themselves before returning to England. Some of them became lost and were never heard from again. But some of those who returned brought with them stories they had heard from the Inuit about starving and mad white men who had begun to feed on one another's flesh.

It is a disturbing and grim tale: it haunts our country like Banquo's ghost, and we seem to be unable to recover from the lure and the horror of it. In 1986, the bodies under the three gravestones were exhumed. They were almost perfectly preserved by permafrost, and as a result of the fine photography of Brian Spenceley, a descendant of one of the men, who had been brought along as the official photographer for archaeologist Owen Beattie's research trip, we were able to look into the faces of three young men from the nineteenth century. They looked a great deal like our own sons and brothers, and in some quiet, unspoken way the whole nation grieved for them.

Then, in 2014, after much effort on the part of the Canadian Coast Guard, Franklin's ship the *Erebus* was found on the ocean floor not far from Beechey Island. But this discovery, exciting and important though it was, lacked the human touch of the isolated graves. Those three young sailors from over a hundred years ago, into whose faces, miraculously, we were able to gaze, came to represent all young men who, through their own natural curiosity and enthusiasm, end up in wars and jobs and explorations that kill them far too soon.

Canoe

BY THE TIME I WAS NINE YEARS OLD, I HAD received my badge for Intermediate Canoeing. This meant that I could name all the parts of a canoe, perform the various strokes necessary for speed and navigation, recite all canoe-related safety rules (never stand up in a canoe!), portage over wild terrain (with help), and pull up to a dock without scraping or bumping. I had already paddled dozens of miles, learned all the canoeing libretto, and made a couple of oil paintings while sitting cross-legged on the bottom of a canoe with my back resting against an uncomfortable thwart. I had also pulled away from human comforts in a small fleet of five canoes and—in the company of children my own age, under the supervision of a couple of fourteen-year-olds—gone "into the wild" for a period of four days, during which I paddled all day long, lived on nothing but beans and marshmallows, and slept in the open (once under a canoe while a thunderstorm raged in the heavens above). This was because, like many Canadian children, I was sent north by my parents to camp in the summer.

My father in particular had insisted on this. He had a great love for the waterways of Canada and the wild landscapes that existed beyond the shorelines of these waterways. As a young teenager, he had paddled with a friend from their home on the Bay of Quinte through the entire 240 miles of the Trent–Severn Waterway to Georgian Bay and back again. Shortly after that legendary summer ended, a mining engineer spoke at an assembly at my father's high school in Trenton, Ontario, and right then and there, my father knew for sure what he wanted to do with his life.

My father's own father had died in the 1918 influenza pandemic, leaving behind a wife and four young children. It would not be easy for my father to go to the University of Toronto's School of Mining, but by working in a city grocery store, applying persistence, and enduring poverty (he also sent money home to his family), he managed to do just that. It was enormously important to him. It was his ticket back to the northern landscapes that he had fallen in love with while paddling a canoe.

The canoe was the craft—at one time the only craft, as the aboriginal peoples of Canada knew and continue to know so well—that could take you to certain remote parts of this country. The fact that the fur and timber trades developed at all came down to the existence of canoes, along with the presence of aboriginal guides who taught the Europeans how to build and paddle them. The mining business would be no different, and there are many stories of precious metals being discovered by men in canoes, and sometimes even by men falling out of canoes. The discovery of the vein that led to the establishment of Little Long Lac Gold Mine—the reason I was born in the Diocese of Moosonee—was a case in point. My father said that prospector Tom Johnson was so excited when he saw what looked to be a gold vein under the waters of Kenogamisis Lake, he broke the safety rules, stood up, and fell out of his canoe. When he surfaced, he reported to his mate—trapper Tony Oklend, who was sitting dumbstruck in the stern—that the vein got better and better the deeper it went. The mine, when it was built, operated mostly under the lake.

Pierre Elliott Trudeau, the very polished and very intellectual fifteenth prime minister of Canada, would choose for the cover of his autobiography a photo of himself in the buckskin jacket he wore while canoeing. This was because, like my father, he was most himself when experiencing the outdoor wilderness life offered by the rivers and lakes of the North.

Trudeau was passionate about canoe trips, not only because of the places they took him, but because of the psychological transformation they could engender. As he

himself put it in "Exhaustion and Fulfilment: The Ascetic in a Canoe," an essay he wrote when he was twenty-five years old, there is something transformative about a journey of this kind, and "it purifies you more rapidly and inescapably than any other.... For it is a condition of such a trip that you entrust yourself, stripped of your worldly goods, to nature."

I remember being nine years old, camping on a rocky island in the middle of a choppy lake, huddled under a canoe in my increasingly wet sleeping bag while thunder seemed to be somersaulting through the air. And I remember the next morning as well—the teenaged counsellors discussing their boyfriends beside the fire, the soggy bread that became delicious toast in a world washed clean, and the equally delicious and utter absence of a city world run by adults.

Back in that city world, during long winter nights when I was awakened by the sound of urban snowploughs, I would visualize the rippling water beside a summer canoe. The dark gold of a submerged paddle would come into my mind, and I would recall that an entire change of direction could be effected simply by a turn of my wrist. How strange and wondrous that thought would seem in a season of rules, timetables, and obedience.

Bird Feeder

ON A FRIGID DAY IN LATE JANUARY, WHEN the whole world is white and beautifully inert, one begins to imagine that death will be painted—as it was for the members of the Franklin expedition—in the same way the icy winter landscape is presenting itself outside the window. Everything will be wincingly precise: there will be no subtleties and no variation. All will be frozen into unblemished place forever and ever and ever. The white will be a perfect shade of white, and the sky will be a perfect shade of Virgin Mary blue. The season itself will never, ever change. And then, in the midst of this thought, a chickadee swings into one's line of vision, grabs a seed from the feeder, and loops back out—a tiny heartbeat, a little hopeful burst of life. A cardinal or a blue jay might follow, bossy and arrogant, shocking in its brazenly hued feathers. These birds have no

intention of letting the winter take their breath away. They live here. They are here to stay.

When many of their cousins have decamped to Florida or California, some birds still have the courage to over-winter in Canada. Their feathers are filled with down pockets that trap and warm air, and their hearts—built with four small chambers—are set to beat faster and faster in order to keep their body temperature from fluctuating. Like us, they are endothermic—warm-blooded—so their high body temperature does not vary regardless of the weather. When it is particularly cold, they will sometimes huddle for warmth.

The appearance of an angel in the backyard would be a surprise. But truly, an angel is a quite ordinary former human being, with a human-shaped body, attempting to be a bird. Birds, in all their variety, their spontaneous manifestations, their plumage, and their songs, are truly a wonder. Their morning song is sometimes not as loud and glorious as it was, and some species of birds are under serious threat. Still, Canadians believe in the miracle of birds, and we feed them in the winter to keep the miracle alive.

Memorial

A YEAR OR SO AFTER THE FIRST WORLD WAR ended, an appeal for donations appeared in the *Stratford Beacon Herald*, in Stratford, Ontario. "Did you lose a pal in the War?" was the header, followed in slightly smaller print by these words:

By death they gave us life. Nearly three hundred of those from Stratford and surrounding Townships, after months or years of hardship, danger and sacrifice, sealed with their blood and their lives, their devotion to our country and to us—their friends.

The appeal goes on to command readers to "THINK! THINK of your friends who sleep in Flanders Fields, and GIVE GENEROUSLY to Stratford's War Memorial."

And give they did. The people of this small city, barely

more than a town of fifteen thousand at the time, opened their hearts and their pocketbooks.

Stratford was then, and to a certain extent still remains, a working-class town. By 1920, when this appeal began, one-fifth of all the furniture manufactured in Canada was made there, and the Grand Trunk Railway, which had established its locomotive shops in Stratford in the 1870s, still employed almost half of the town's population. Stratford was also an important railroad hub—with trains departing for the west and the east of Canada, and tracks heading southwest to Chicago—and this made the shipment of furniture and manufactured goods very convenient.

Donations from workers arrived daily at city hall—one, two, occasionally even ten dollars—sometimes with touching notes attached. *This is because of my friend Jim.* Or, *My brother died, though I came back.* Often, however, factory owners sent in a list of employees with a record of how much was donated by each worker, the company itself claiming credit for the grand total on the bottom line. One can imagine the sense of obligation and guilt attached to such a list making the rounds of a noisy factory. But one can also imagine the palpable absence of the many who had left behind steady jobs on the assembly line to answer the mother country's call only five or six years before and had never returned.

And then there were the men from the outlying townships, farm boys who had completed their last day of chores and walked to town to enlist. Girls from these rural outskirts sent in a dollar. Mothers often sent their egg money, along with a pencilled note regarding their love for a deceased son, occasionally two. Men who sent money often spelled their son's name in uppercase letters, followed by the words "my boy."

In many ways, the resulting memorial was like many built in Canada from coast to coast to coast in the years following the Great War, as it was then called. I have seen, for example, the book that contains the minutes from the memorial committee of the village of Castleton. My grandfather was chair of that committee. Lists of the dead were drawn up and chiselled into stone from Truro, Nova Scotia, to Nanaimo, British Columbia. People assembled for the unveiling and wept at their unthinkable losses, then turned their faces away from death and back to their lives. For a while. They returned to these memorials after the Second World War, and again after the Korean War. They added more names.

But in one way the Stratford memorial was different from most of the others.

Stratfordians were fortunate in that among their numbers there was a man dedicated to great public works. R. Thomas Orr was born in the town in 1870 and lived there until his death in 1957, and in that time, he not only established the insurance business that bears his name but also helped to create Stratford's gorgeous parklands (which would provide the setting for the Stratford Shakespearean Festival in 1953),

the public library, the Upper Thames River Conservation Authority, and the Stratford Historical Society. He was a man with a keen sense of which people to seek out when there was a civic need of a cultural nature. He contacted Frederick G. Todd, who had trained with the firm of Frederick Law Olmsted (of Central Park fame), when he needed someone to design the park system along the river; he wrote to Andrew Carnegie when he wanted to see a library in the town; and when it came time to plan the war memorial, he asked Walter Allward if he would be willing to submit a design. All three men complied.

The memorial is not only a fitting tribute to the young people of Stratford and surroundings who lost their lives in the wars, but also an important work of art that becomes more powerful each time it is visited. All of Allward's memorials pay attention to the tragedy (rather than the glory) of war and the grief that follows. The two bronze figures on the plinth combine strength with sorrow.

After they had been in contact for some time, R. Thomas Orr wrote to Allward concerning the progress of the town's cenotaph. At the bottom of the letter, having just read the paper, Orr congratulated the sculptor for having received a commission to create a huge memorial to the dead and missing Canadians in France—a memorial that, he understood, was to be erected on the edge of Vimy Ridge.

Cherry Tree

I WAS JUST A TODDLER IN JUNE 1953 AT THE TIME of the coronation of Queen Elizabeth II. I remember very little about the celebratory parade representing various groups that passed down the main street of Geraldton, Ontario, near where my family was living at the time. One inner picture remains bright, however: a float filled with paper cherry blossoms blooming on the end of elaborately constructed, life-sized paper trees. Among these trees drifted slim, lovely, kimono-clad, parasol-carrying women who, now and then, bowed gracefully to the crowd.

The question that I wouldn't have asked at the time was how a small Japanese-Canadian community had come to be in what was then considered a remote part of Northern Ontario. Sadly, the answer to this question sheds light on what is one of the most shameful acts of Canada's past.

In 1942, during the Second World War and after the

declaration of war on Japan, twenty-one thousand Canadians of Japanese descent (75 percent of whom were born in Canada, and some of whom had served in the First World War) were declared security threats and enemy aliens by the government of Prime Minister Mackenzie King. Under the War Measures Act, the removal of all Japanese Canadians living within one hundred miles of the Pacific coast was carried out. They were taken from their homes; their property was seized, sold, and never returned; and they were placed in detention centres and internment camps, or sent as unpaid workers to factory farms. One of the "road camps" created to carve out or maintain the highways that joined the part of Northern Ontario where I lived with the cities to the south was situated not that far from the street on which I stood watching that coronation parade.

The war had been over for eight years in 1953, and the detention centres and internment camps were closed. But their legacy lived on. Shockingly, the Japanese Canadians who had been so unjustly treated were still not welcome on the coast of their home province of British Columbia. Moreover, since their homes and property, their businesses and fishing boats had been seized and sold, there was nothing much to return to anyway. So some of them decided to settle in the regions of their internment.

Six-year-old Joy (Nakayama) Kogawa was living in Vancouver with her brother and her parents when the federal government confiscated her home at 1450 West 64th Avenue and sent her family to an internment camp at Slocan, in the interior of British Columbia. Years later, in 2003, after she had become a writer and had published her award-winning novel, *Obasan*, which deals with this appalling period of our history, Joy visited her old neighbourhood and noticed that the house where she had spent her early childhood was for sale, with the cherry tree she had loved as a child still growing in the backyard. Two years later, after much hard work on the part of the Save Joy Kogawa House Committee and help from the Land Conservancy of British Columbia, the Historic Joy Kogawa House was purchased and turned into a writer's retreat.

By then, the original cherry tree was dying. Happily, however, two new trees were able to be grown from a cutting taken from the old. The first of these was planted in the backyard, where schoolchildren who have read Kogawa's *Naomi's Tree* are often brought to see it. The second grows at Vancouver City Hall, where it was planted by Joy and Councillor Jim Green on a day in November that would come to be known as Obasan Cherry Tree Day. Everyone in the city calls these cherry saplings the Friendship Trees.

When I look into my memory now, I realize that what I took away from the Northern Ontario version of Coronation Day 1953 was the sense of a delicate, fragile world of paper flowers and courteous gestures that had appeared as if by

magic on the otherwise unrefined main street of a rough, hastily assembled town that serviced a number of surrounding mining sites. Only a toddler, I had no idea of the pain and humiliation that had brought such strong and gracious people to the place where I was born.

Tent

BECAUSE THERE WAS LITTLE TO NO WORK FOR a Catholic in the Northern Ireland of his youth, Danny Henry came to Canada as a young man in the early 1930s. He sought and found employment in Toronto as one in a team of Irish labourers who were hired to build Maple Leaf Gardens, and who subsequently worked digging tunnels under the lake for what is now known as the R.C. Harris Water Treatment Plant. The experience that the team members earned in such a setting led to them being hired out as shaft and development miners for the new mines that were being constructed north of Lake Superior in the mid-1930s, and this was how Danny met my father and became his best friend, and how, a decade and a half later, he became my godfather.

After he had worked on the construction of the mine

under Kenogamisis Lake (but long before I was born), Danny's interests turned to prospecting, a profession for which he was well suited. A great favourite with women, Danny nevertheless enjoyed the single—and on occasion even solitary—life. His great physical strength and genial confidence made cutting trail and making camp a breeze for him, and he loved adventure, discovery, and the notion of luck.

Tents have been a part of human life for thousands of years—as long, it seems, as people sought to find ways to keep heat, cold, and inclement weather out of their lives. The nomadic First Peoples of North America, and even those more settled, had beautifully decorated skin tents, often constructed with a smoke hole at the top so a fire could be made at the centre. These skin tents could be dismantled and set up again with relative ease, using the branches of nearby trees for poles and pegs, and windfall limbs and twigs for firewood. They could also be carried on journeys from one place to another.

In December and January of 1953–54, Danny Henry set out for Manitouwadge Lake on what would become a forty-one-day staking trip, and with him he of course took his prospector's tent (or walled tent, as they are sometimes called). He also took a small Quebec wood stove, cooking utensils, and a fellow prospector, Jack Peet—a very good thing, in that the amount of gear being carried would have made the trek close to impossible for a man travelling on his own. Even so, it took the pair six days to walk the ten miles from where the train let them off to the site of the rumoured "strike." Never once did the temperature rise above twenty-five below, and on occasion it dropped as low as fifty below. But each night the tent would be pitched, snow would be shovelled out the front flap, the fire would be lit, and the two would be quite comfortable in their Arctic sleeping bags.

Not so some of the speculators from the city who followed in Danny and Jack's footsteps. Though most of the men who subsequently staked claims in what became known as the Big Rush would have had tents of their own, one person from the city, dressed in a bow tie and Oxford shoes, leapt out of a hired bush plane that had been outfitted with skis and, to Danny's great amusement, began enthusiastically staking claims with his ungloved hands. "The weather was about 30 below, and the snow was 4 feet deep," Danny told the *Fort William Daily Times-Journal*. "He didn't stick it out very long."

But Danny did stick it out. He went back into the bush— not only to the Manitouwadge rush, but all over Canada— with energy and enthusiasm, trip after trip after trip. It wasn't until he was in his late sixties that he hung up his snowshoes, had a huge farewell party at the prospectors convention at the Royal York Hotel in Toronto, and got married for the first (and only) time to Norah Doherty, an Irishwoman from Donegal.

Until this marriage, our house was always home base for Danny. I can still recall the time that he and Dad searched frantically through the belongings Danny had left with us, looking for the shares he'd received for working on Maple Leaf Gardens—shares that had boomed in the intervening years. They found them, and Danny, who had never in his life owned property, used his good fortune to buy a house near his birthplace in Kilrea, Northern Ireland.

When both my father and my mother had died (Danny had predeceased them), my brothers found Danny's prospecting gear in our parents' attic: several picks and sample bags, snowshoes, Arctic parkas and down-filled sleeping bags, a Coleman stove, backpacks, the small tin wood stove that heated his tent, and the wonderful prospector's tent itself. This last item was folded neatly and tied, as if it were patiently waiting to be carried back into the bush and pitched—and heated—once again. For over forty years, that tent had been Danny's only real Canadian home.

Danceland

A FRIEND ONCE TOLD ME THAT PEOPLE FROM the Prairies—especially those who live in Saskatchewan—love their vehicles and think nothing of driving them for very long distances. You can see farther on the Prairies than anywhere else in the world, my friend assured me, and you can drive farther as well. "Hell," he said, "anyone I know would drive a hundred miles or so just to purchase a hamburger, never mind how far they would go to get to a dance hall. They'd drive all day and night to get to a dance hall."

At Manitou Beach, near Watrous, Saskatchewan, there were once three dance halls jumping with music and revellers all weekend long. The lake is said to have curative properties, which explains its allure to the medical tourists of the turn of the century, but by the 1920s and 1930s, it was all striped bathing costumes and wild dancing into the

night, preceded and followed by the kind of madcap auto-mobile journeys that would not have been unfamiliar to F. Scott Fitzgerald's Jay Gatsby. Young people poured in from Regina and Saskatoon, one hundred miles away. Sometimes they came from as far as Calgary or Winnipeg. They danced in the afternoons, cooled off in the waters of the lake, then danced all evening long. On Sundays, when dancing was forbidden, they sat in their cars and waited until the halls opened for the Sunday Midnight Frolic, at which point they danced until 4 a.m. on what was essentially Monday morning.

Only one of these dance halls has survived to the present day—the much-celebrated cathedral of dance called Danceland. Built out of Douglas fir, with a vaulted timber ceiling lifted by exposed wooden trusses, Danceland is a hallowed, sacred space one gains access to through the large double doors in the centre of its arched exterior. But what really makes the building come alive is its maple dance floor. The bounce of this "floating floor," which is fitted overtop of twenty tons of tightly packed horsetail hair, has always caused couples to levitate in each other's arms. Over the years, men and women have danced to the marvellous horns and strings of such well-known big bands as the Harmony Seven and Mark Kenny and His Western Gentlemen. There are also Danceland rumours concerning everyone who matters—Ella Fitzgerald sang here, Duke Ellington played, Glenn Miller and his band were said to have detoured from Chattanooga just to see the floating floor, and Hank Snow apparently arrived one winter night with a sidekick named Elvis in tow. And then there are the images made by that great Prairie artist David Thauberger, who has immortalized Danceland in his iconic paintings and prints, which have become known, along with the rest of his work, all over North America.

I've often thought that Saskatchewan would have been the perfect subject for one of *New Yorker* cartoonist Saul Steinberg's brilliant, spare—almost empty—maps. On it would be the two discrete cities of Regina and Saskatoon, the marvellous hermitages of St. Peter's Abbey, the tilting sanatorium of Fort San, and of course, Danceland with its arched facade and multicoloured sign. He might have also added the abandoned 1950s radar station where the Saskatchewan Writers' Guild once held its annual summer workshops, and where I myself taught a couple of decades ago.

It was from this radar station (as a result of one of those spontaneous driving decisions taken by the people—in this case, the poets—of the Prairies) that I was transported to Danceland on a moonlit summer night. Hell, it's only an hour away, I was told. I recall the flat, straight road illuminated by the headlights of the car, the thick darkness that hid the land out the side windows, the punctuation of stars, and the odd, infrequent yard light of the few farmhouses en route. And then the lights of Danceland with a plethora of pickup trucks in the surrounding parking lot. The trusses of its cathedral ceiling were dressed in spotlit silver paper, and the music of the band demanded physical action. Soon I was experiencing the bounce of the floating floor while I levitated in the arms of one Prairie poet after another.

Skates

SOME OF US HAVE BEEN LUCKY ENOUGH TO LIVE near bodies of water on which it is possible to skate in winter. The Rideau Canal in Ottawa is one such body. On midwinter mornings, it becomes an ice highway on which it is not uncommon to see businessmen, civil servants, teachers, librarians, politicians, and uniformed police officers skating to work. Another such body of water is Wellesley Pond in the village of Wellesley, Ontario. It is possible to skate on that pond by daylight or by moonlight, and possible also to travel farther afield. The thing about millponds is that they are made by damming up a stream or a river. After enjoying the pond itself, you can skate upstream into the mysterious distance, while the frozen creek under your blades becomes thinner, more treed, more interesting. The light of the sun or moon passes through the branches and changes the patterns of what you see, and there is always that sense of having glided into another state of being, of having left the ordinary behind.

There are other sides to skating, of course. There is hockey and the excitement around the Stanley Cup for men's hockey and the more recent wonderful Clarkson Cup for women's hockey. There are gifted figure skaters and the glory of the Olympics, and the memory of the more commercial but still fascinating Ice Capades. But being a secular skater surrounded by fields or forests is an experience to be savoured. There is that unmistakable sound, and sometimes the echo of the sound, of a blade on ice. There is the whiteness of the world that unspools on either side of the creek. There are, sometimes, ice crystals glinting in sun-filled air. There is the knowledge of the dark, liquid world under the ice, where certain weeds still live in winter, and where fish drowse.

If you live on the edge of Wellesley Pond, as I did for almost two decades, sometimes on a winter night, just as you are settling into bed with a book, you will hear soft laughter rising from the ice. When you pull aside the curtain, you will see—to your utter amazement—young girls with long braids, dressed in wool jackets and long gingham skirts, skating on the ice. They link arms and move in pairs around and around the pond, speaking and laughing quietly. These are the Old Order Mennonite girls of the area. Preferring the privacy of semi-darkness, they have come to the village ice—sometimes

by horse and buggy—for a Saturday night treat, and they are beautiful and enigmatic in their discretion and their palpable joy. What an honour it is to see them like this—a suggestion of the past, but still so fully present, and so near, that you can see their breath in the cold night air. Their white tulle bonnets are touched by moonlight, and their dark skates leave elegant patterns that you will walk out to see in the morning, when they have gone.

Innu Tea Doll

I CAN RECALL BEING GIVEN ONLY ONE PRACTICAL toy as a child—a small red snow shovel that I loved fiercely, though I doubt my acts of snow clearing were all that effective. It is still in my possession, however, and has proved handy in my adulthood for getting at those odd narrow areas between the rises of steps or underneath the railings of verandas. But it is undeniably prosaic.

Especially when compared with a toy like the utilitarian and beautiful Innu tea doll.

The Innu of northern Quebec and eastern Labrador are one of the last remaining nomadic, tribal hunting-gathering peoples who, until a few decades ago, possibly because of the remoteness of their territory, were able to thrive in the vast area known to them as Nitassinan, or "the land." Following the caribou—and being dependent on that animal for food, shelter, and clothing—meant travelling great distances on

the one hand and developing well-honed hunting skills on the other. Harvested from a low, shrub-like rhododendron species that grows on the tundra, tea was considered to be both energy-providing and medicinal. These small dolls—no two alike—redolent with personality and expression, were stuffed with tea leaves and transported in the hands of children, who played with them and loved them. When it came time to make tea, the doll's side was opened, the leaves were taken out, and the cloth was stitched back together again. When the tea was gone, the doll was stuffed with leaves and grasses until more tea leaves could be found.

In the early days, the dolls would have been made entirely of caribou skin. Later, after Western contact, bright bits of European cloth were added to their costumes. But the faces continued to be made from animal hide, giving the dolls their character, their look of good humour, and their grace. These are very friendly homunculi, eager to be of service, and at the same time, their smiles make them seem to be aware of providing companionship. The children with whom they travelled would have been very fond of them, and would have had the sense that their love was requited and that the dolls would always be with them, no matter how long the journey.

Horse

THE ROYAL CANADIAN MOUNTED POLICE Musical Ride is an iconic Canadian performance in which Mounties clothed in formal scarlet attire ride black horses in a patterned manner while various jigs, reels, and strathspeys are piped into the ring. Seen from above, the proceedings are like a sort of terrestrial synchronized-swimming sequence. At ground level, however, it is the fierce eyes of the black horses, glaring out from under their frowning foreheads, that one recalls most vividly. Especially if one was a child who was taken each year to see this wonder at Toronto's Royal Agricultural Winter Fair. And especially if, like me, one was a child afraid of horses.

The fierce eyes of a horse that I may very well have seen from the stands in, say, 1959 are still on display, along with the rest of him, in the RCMP Heritage Centre in Regina, Saskatchewan. Nero, Regimental Horse Number 295, was so

beloved by the troop that in 1972, when his time came, he was sent to a taxidermist for preservation. The results were mostly successful. In spite of the fact that—with time—his shiny black coat has faded to a dull brown, his eyes are still disturbingly large and dark, and his demeanour remains proud and, under the circumstances, more than a little indignant.

Nero was not known for his good nature. Nor did he suffer fools. According to legend, he rigorously educated not only the newer horses but also freshman human recruits. The latter being more selfish and stubborn than their animal colleagues, Nero dealt with them in a particularly strict manner, often shaking them off his back as if they were irritating insects and walking disdainfully away. But he knew and loved all the ceremonial manoeuvres, and once the recruits were skilled enough to meet his standards, he treated them with courtesy and occasionally even with kindness.

Nero was born at the RCMP Remount Ranch in Fort Walsh, Saskatchewan, in 1954. Like all RCMP horses, he would have grazed peacefully in sylvan pastures—at least in the warmer months—until he was three years old. Then he would have begun his two-year ceremonial training, which consisted of confidence-building exercises, followed by instruction in the various drills: the Diamond, Threading the Needle, the Bridal Arch, the Dome, the Lance, and those three immortal favourites, the Shanghai Cross, the Shanghai Double Cross, and the Shanghai Double

Crossover. Eventually, at the age of five and a half, weighing somewhere between a thousand and fourteen hundred pounds, and standing somewhere between sixteen and seventeen hands, Nero would have made his stage debut.

To my way of thinking, however, there is a dark side to Nero and his ilk. I can see him in my mind's eye, silhouetted against a storm-tossed sky, rearing up in a Fuseli-like nightmare, or perhaps, like one of those terrifying battle-crazed horses from a painting by Géricault or Delacroix, tossing his mane in rage. Not every Musical Ride horse had a white spot on his forehead. But Nero did. And it accentuated his eyes, the wildness in them, making me fear—and admire—him even more.

Neon

I HAVE ALWAYS LOVED THE NAME "LAKE OF THE Woods." Something about the placement of the words brings to mind a large, dark oval covering a drowned medieval forest. Almost as intriguing is the apparent need to explain or translate the name, and the several competing narratives that have come into being as a result. Some say it came from French fur traders, who were so often lost among its fourteen thousand heavily treed islands that they called it Lac du Bois. Others, unwilling to ignore the staggering quantity of islands, claim it is a mistranslation of *minitie*, an Ojibwa word meaning "lake of the islands." *The Canadian Encyclopedia* agrees that the name arose from a mistranslation of an "Indian word," but insists that the word meant "inland lake of the hills." It is a lake that refuses to commit and settle down, and so it is fitting that it belongs to Manitoba, Ontario, and Minnesota. To make things even

more complicated, the lake itself is a ghost, a shadow, a faint memory of a former glacial lake called Agassiz.

Added to all this romance is the mystery of Five Roses. In 1888, a handful of railway barons founded a major enterprise called the Lake of the Woods Milling Company on the northwestern Ontario side of the lake. And then, some years later, they changed the company's name to Five Roses Flour. Eventually, they moved the headquarters of Five Roses to Montreal, thereby losing the Lake of the Woods connection altogether.

What is now known as the Five Roses sign in Montreal began its life, like Lake of the Woods, with a completely different name. In the 1940s, the Montreal silo of Ogilvie Flour Mills was surmounted by a large, red bilingual neon sign that blinked the words "Farine Ogilvie Flour" into the night sky. In the 1950s, when Ogilvie bought out the Lake of the Woods Milling Company, the sign was changed to "Farine Five Roses Flour." Finally, when Quebec was visited by the Quiet Revolution and subsequent language laws in the 1960s and 1970s, the word *flour* was removed. Because it was part of a logo, the English word *five* was permitted to remain.

Words have power. We change and rearrange them to suit our purposes. Now that Ogilvie itself no longer exists, the future of the iconic sign is in question. With time, a few of the letters of this familiar night fixture of the Montreal skyline have grown faint as the various tubes of neon burn out. Blink after blink after blink.

Something is always lost in translation.

Torah

MY FATHER WAS BORN IN HASTINGS COUNTY, Ontario, in the town of Deseronto, which is situated on Lake Ontario's Bay of Quinte. According to him, his forebears on both sides had lived in the Deseronto area (and in Prince Edward County, across the bay) for several generations before his arrival. My father loved Prince Edward County and Hastings County equally, and could recite the townships of both, backwards and forwards in rapid succession—something he did with panache at parties. He also told stories of iceboating on the bay as a teenager and courting in a canoe during the dog days of summer. His family name was Carter, but there were Saylors in his background and, on his mother's side, Weisses. Saylor was an old Prince Edward County name, and so was Weese, but spelled with a double *e*, not the way my grandmother's maiden name was spelled.

After 1900, my grandfather, Newbold Carter, ran a chain of leather goods stores in the principal towns of Prince Edward and Hastings counties, something he continued to do until he died of influenza in 1918. This early death, and then, a couple of decades later, the death of his wife, Gertrude Weiss, meant that my brothers and I grew up knowing very little about that side of the family. Although my parents attended the local Anglican church, there was always some question about my grandmother's family heritage. Was it possible that her ancestors had been Jewish?

Some members of the family, citing the predominantly Scots and English settlers of Loyalist Prince Edward and Hastings counties, said it couldn't possibly be so. Weiss was a German name, they contended—which is of course true, but that does not answer the Jewish question. Others seemed to remember hearing something vague about Hungary and distant forebears leaving that country for the new land.

It was with all this in mind that I began to look into Jewish settlements in the predominantly Protestant vicinity of Prince Edward County and Hastings County, hoping to find some information about the grandmother I never knew. I was not successful in my search for my grandmother, but I came across other stories in my research—one of which delighted me for all kinds of reasons.

Belleville is a place that I have most often associated with *Life in the Clearings versus the Bush*, a non-fiction book by

Susanna Moodie, who wrote and published lively autobiographical works about her years in pioneer Upper Canada. I also associate the town with the nearby Trenton air base, and the fact that the beautiful Moira River enters Lake Ontario there. One thing I never thought about over the years was Belleville's synagogue—the miracle, in fact, of its existence in one of the most thoroughly WASP regions of Southern Ontario.

As it turns out, Belleville was not as WASP as I (and everyone I knew) assumed. One of its earliest and most influential citizens, George Benjamin, was most certainly of Jewish descent, in spite of the fact that he was a powerful member of the local Orange Lodge in the 1830s. He later became a politician in the then entirely WASP Conservative Party and may have practised the Jewish faith in a private way. He also contributed enormously to the prestige of the town by founding the well-known paper *The Weekly Intelligencer* in 1834.

A few decades later there were Jewish furriers and peddlers living in the town, and a number of Jewish travelling salesmen passing through. Eventually, in 1905, two members of the Jewish community set up the Mary Street Home for Jewish Workers as a boarding house for travelling Jews who were in search of a kosher meal. It was in this former rolling mill turned rooming house that the first Jewish religious services were held. But as more Jewish merchants moved to town and the congregation increased in size, the community began to rent the Orange Hall for Friday night Shabbat

services. Finally, in 1929, a house on Pinnacle Street was converted to the Sons of Jacob synagogue, and the first Torah was presented to the congregation by Julius Samuels (who had lived in Belleville all his life and owned a local junkyard). A long succession of warm and devoted people had led their friends, relatives, and neighbours to this moment. The new synagogue would provide a home not only for the Jewish community of Belleville and surroundings, but also for visiting Jewish servicemen at the nearby air base, whose numbers were to increase significantly in the not-too-distant future during the Second World War.

It is the story of the transfer of the Torah to the Ark in the synagogue that same year, however, that I find even more heartwarming and delightful than all the life-enhancing stories that preceded it and have followed it. All of WASP Belleville apparently came out to see the parade: some had decorated their vehicles and actively participated. And most wonderfully, the music for the procession was provided by the Belleville Salvation Army band with all their instruments trumpeting and blazing in the sun.

A few years ago, when my daughter had her DNA tested, she discovered that she is 7 percent Middle Eastern and most probably Jewish.

Whale Bucket

THE THULE, WHO LIKELY MIGRATED OVER THE Bering Strait and across Alaska a thousand years ago, were the ancestors of the Canadian Inuit people of the coastal Arctic. They, and their many generations of Inuit grandchildren, were skilled hunters, especially when it came to a mammal as impressive in stature and as essential to their culture as the bowhead whale. The bowhead was everything to such cultures: it was food and clothing and shelter; it was tools and toys and watercraft. During the long, dark winters, it was not only legend and music and education, but also the rafters above (which were made from the ribs of the whale) and the lamplight in which the stories and songs and lessons were passed on.

There was the story of the raven that flew into the mouth of a whale. He continued flying down the whale's throat to the centre of the animal, where he found a woman tending a lamp. The woman appeared and withdrew, appeared and withdrew, always keeping the lamp lit. When the raven asked why she came and went so regularly, the woman answered with two words: "Breath," she said, "life." In this way the raven knew that the woman was the soul of the whale, and the breath, and that the lamp she kept lit was the whale's heart.

The many lessons an Inuit child learned were connected to affection and respect. If one did not respect the whale, it would not make itself available for human consumption. As such, it was necessary to wear new clothing when going to a hunt, and to speak in soft, discreet tones, keeping all calm and quiet. Kayaks, rather than the larger skin boats called umiaks, were used, not for their stealth but for their peacefulness.

Inuit believed that the whale itself would select the hunter it wanted to be harpooned by: not just anyone would be skilled or pure enough. They also believed, and continue to believe, that to fail to use every aspect of the whale's anatomy was disrespectful and would result in there being no whale to hunt in the following season. Over-hunting would lead to the disappearance of the whales, but so would no hunting, as it was believed to be disrespectful not to "harvest" a whale that had made itself available to enable human life.

Many talismans and charms and carvings were made from whalebones and were attached to the harpoons and knives and other instruments used in the hunt. Often a

bucket decorated with such works of art would be brought along as well. Inuit were aware that although the whale lived in the sea, it was dependent on oxygen. Salt water could never, therefore, quench its thirst. As a final act of respect, then, the hunters would offer the newly killed whale a drink of fresh water from the ceremonial bucket, and further seasons of successful hunting would be assured.

Medal

LESTER BOWLES PEARSON WAS ONE OF THE FEW Canadian leaders who could be thought of as a genuine *public servant*, in that almost everything he did—or tried to do—was truly for the greater public good. He was a Liberal politician who became (from 1963 to 1968) the fourteenth prime minister of Canada, and while he was in office, his government adopted the Canada Pension Plan, the universal medicare system, and the maple leaf flag that is a recognized Canadian symbol all over the planet. But even before he became prime minister, Pearson made a significant contribution to the betterment of the globe. If Canada is known around the world as a nation of peace-keepers—whether or not this is a fully accurate view of our activities—this is largely due to the accomplishments of this one distinguished Canadian.

Already enrolled at the University of Toronto, Pearson

was only eighteen years old when, in 1915, during the Great War, he joined the Canadian Army Medical Corps and became a stretcher-bearer in Greece. This could only have been a life-changing experience for this son of a Canadian Methodist minister—an introduction to the horrors of war that would have been impossible to forget. He was invalided out in 1917 as the result of an accident rather than a military event, however, and he returned to the university, completing his BA in advance of graduate work at Oxford. He came back to the University of Toronto to teach history for a short while, and then joined the Canadian government's Department of External Affairs.

It is interesting to consider that Pearson's was a generation of returned veterans: almost everyone he studied with, taught with, and worked with would have carried images from the Armageddon of that chaotic, brutal war around with them in their visual memories. Mostly unarticulated, these horrific memories would be something the veterans held in common as a group. They also would have understood that their wartime experiences were incomprehensible to the generations who preceded and followed them, as well as everyone who had stayed at home. Being a stretcher-bearer would have put Pearson at the epicentre of pain. There were no words to describe it. Lester Pearson, in his own mild way, wanted to fix it. He wanted to ensure it would never happen again.

It would, of course: war was always breaking out here

and there, over and over again. There was barely time to recover from the First World War before the Second World War happened, and that was then followed by the Cold War and all the crises that attended it. As a child I was very aware of these crises, and their potential to finish off the world altogether. There was always the suggestion that in some suburb or another, just out of range (and therefore of no use to me and my family when the catastrophe occurred), people were building bomb shelters. The notion of "nuclear fallout" was widely discussed. Communists were seen as agents of the devil, and Russians, in particular, were to be fully distrusted.

The 1956 Suez Crisis was the event that made Pearson's reputation. Both Britain and France were enormously dependent on the Suez Canal in Egypt to facilitate the delivery of oil to their ports. When Egypt's president, Gamal Abdel Nasser, nationalized the canal, these nations became alarmed and retaliated by taking military action with the help of their regional ally, Israel. Egypt, in turn, sought aid from the USSR. Americans, Canadians, and other NATO members felt that world peace was being threatened. France and Britain were ordered by the United Nations to withdraw.

It was Canada's secretary of state for external affairs, Lester Pearson, who, to deal with the crisis, facilitated the creation of the United Nations' first peacekeeping force. After some delicate negotiations, and with full UN backing, a ceasefire occurred and all three aggressors withdrew from Egypt and

the canal, allegedly with their pride intact. The truth, however, was much more decisive: Britain, already weakened by two world wars, would never again be the world leader it had once been.

Pearson was awarded the Nobel Peace Prize in 1957 for his diplomatic genius. Rarely has a federal Cabinet minister been so respected outside our borders. Back at home, however, reviews were mixed. There were many who accused Pearson of abandoning the mother country in her hour of need. Some even used the word *treason*. Pearson, who had seen an entire generation damaged by responding to the mother country in her hour of need, and who had been attempting to establish a world accord with the creation of a peacekeeping force for which Canada is known to this day, was distrusted by a collective still clinging to the notion of imperialism. Astonishingly, at this brilliant moment, the Liberal Party, for which Pearson served, was soundly defeated in the 1957 Canadian federal election, and John Diefenbaker's Conservative majority government was born. My mother, a staunch Liberal, was outraged. "It just goes to show you," she told me the morning after the election, as she angrily stirred the oatmeal on the stove, "Canadians are simply *unable* to accept a compliment."

Tiger

I T SAYS QUITE A LOT ABOUT THE BRITISH EMPIRE
that this tiger-skin rug is situated on the wall of the
Bengal Lounge of the Empress Hotel in Victoria, British
Columbia, some eight thousand miles away from the place
where the poor tiger was born. It is also almost impossible,
these days, to believe that the location of anything—especially
a North American anything—could contain so many refer-
ences to Britain, empire, colonies, and queens. And then there
is this exotic, irrevocably skinned animal thrown into the mix.
But facts are facts. As we know from the fur trade, where
hides were like gold, hunted wildlife was a significant aspect
of Canadian history, and as we can see from the tiger, animal
skins were important in the history of the British Empire
as well.

The Empress is one of series of palace-like hotels built
in the nineteenth and early twentieth centuries by the

Canadian Pacific Railway. Looking back, the creation of these behemoths in an essentially wilderness country (only a half a century old then, and with a total population hovering somewhere around five million) seems as insane and surreal as Mad King Ludwig's fantasy architecture in Bavaria. But the railway was eager to encourage tourists to travel to the western portions of the country, and in 1888, the first two giants—the Hotel Vancouver and the Banff Springs Hotel—opened for business. It is said that the latter was built to resemble a Scottish baronial castle.

Even larger—more fortress than castle—the Empress probably takes its name from the fact that when it was conceived, Queen Victoria (who was also empress of India) had recently died and needed memorializing. The hotel is situated on Vancouver Island, in the small city of Victoria (also named after the queen), and was opened in 1908, and enlarged in 1910 and again in 1928, making one wonder if these repeated expansions were not also part of the empire theme.

The life story of the tiger whose skin became this hanging rug is lost to us. "In what distant deeps or skies / Burnt the fire of thine eyes?" we, like William Blake, may very well ask. There is no doubt, however, that he or she was one of many killed for sport in the tens of thousands of hunts carried out before, after, and most particularly during the British Raj period in India (that is, from 1858 to 1947, during the colonial rule of the British Empire on the Indian subcontinent).

The numbers of "kills" during this time was simply stagger-ing, and led to a decline in tiger population that continues to this day (as does the exploitation and poaching of remaining tigers). So the skin attached to the wall of a large hotel on Vancouver Island has more in common with Canada than one might think. Like the North American buffalo, which grazed in such vast numbers on the western plains of what would become Canada, the tigers of India are victims of what can only be described as human greed, and they are in dan-ger of disappearing altogether.

Snowman

IN SPITE OF THE FACT THAT SOUTHERN BRITISH Columbia sees it only on faraway mountaintops and no more than a couple of times a season, it would be safe to say that all Canadians are, at least for some portion of the year, fully obsessed by snow. They hate it when they are walkers and drivers, and they love it when they are skiers and bobsledders. They build snow forts and igloos and hotels out of it, and they make paths through it and angels in it. Some of them, who want their Christmases to be white, are comforted by the softly falling snow of December. Others are fond of quoting Voltaire's assertion that when looked at in the *cold* light of day, Canada is nothing more than "*quelques arpents de neige.*" And each year a couple of Canadians drop dead of massive heart attacks while they are outside in the cold of January, trying to shovel this *neige* out of the way.

Beardmore, Ontario, situated 125 miles north of Thunder

Bay, has taken a positive attitude toward snow. After making the claim that it holds the title for Snow Capital of the World, this sparsely populated mining and lumber town, from which most of the miners and lumberjacks have fled, decided to celebrate its status by building a white wooden structure professing to be the world's largest snowman. This particular Big-Thing-Along-the-Road is unusual even in such an unusual category, in that he is not only the biggest but also the longest lasting of his ilk. That is, if one defines his ilk as his fellow snowmen, and ignores the fact that he has been torn down and replaced at least once.

Over the years, the snowman has been both a tourist information booth and a temporary home for certain patrons of the Beardmore Lounge (who apparently have a key and are rumoured to sometimes sleep it off inside the snowman before going home to face the ire of their women). He has also changed somewhat in his latest incarnation, and now wears sunglasses day and night, winter and summer.

The snowman is not Beardmore's only claim to fame. The town is also the home of one of Canada's most notorious archaeological finds.

During the 1930s, while Beardmore was coming into being, hundreds of prospectors, both amateur and professional (my father among them), were drawn to the region by news of the gold strike at Little Long Lac Gold Mine. One of these prospectors claimed to have found a different kind of gold when he was wandering through the forest: a broken sword and an axe-head that were clearly of ancient origin. The Royal Ontario Museum became involved, and news of the Beardmore Relics, supposed evidence of a Viking settlement halfway between James Bay and Lake Superior, was made known to the public. Soon all Canadian schoolchildren knew the story: how the Vikings had sailed into Hudson Bay in their longboats; how they had proceeded through James Bay and along a complicated series of rivers, reaching the ancient site of Beardmore before the snowman had even been heard of. Eventually unmasked as the hoaxes they were (the "discoverer" had Norwegian friends in Thunder Bay, and one of them had inherited the artefacts from a relative), the relics nevertheless had a profound effect on Canada's collective psyche. Scholars wrote papers, geographers mapped navigable rivers, and a couple of decades later, Farley Mowat, one of Canada's most popular writers, wrote a thrilling young adult novel called *The Curse of the Viking Grave*.

When all is said and done, however, the most important fact about Beardmore is that it is the birthplace of one of Canada's most distinguished painters, Norval Morrisseau (also known as Copper Thunderbird), an Anishinaabe artist from the nearby Sand Point First Nation. Using images from the natural world and from the mystical legends of his people, Morrisseau spent his life (March 14, 1932–December 4, 2007)

creating bright, compelling paintings filled with colour and vitality. As his renown spread, these works of art became much sought after by collectors in the cities to the south, and the demand for his work grew to a sometimes unmanageable degree. In spite of this and a number of personal tragedies, Morrisseau remained focused on the beauty and spirituality of the birds and animals that he remembered from his childhood. All his paintings are warm, pulsing with life, and exuding natural purpose. There is not even a suggestion in them of the cold coming winter, and not a hint of snow.

Microphone

A COUNTRY CAN HAVE A VOICE, AND IF ONE IS fortunate, that voice will inform, delight, entertain, and most important, present vital issues from multiple points of view. The opposite of this is, of course, propaganda. Any collective voice is susceptible to infiltration and politicization, but with vigilance, that danger can be sidelined and minimized. From the beginnings of the Canadian Broadcasting Corporation in the early 1930s, the Canadian government, while funding the Crown corporation the nat-ional broadcaster became in 1936, has at least paid lip service to the notion that an arm's-length relationship should be kept intact, particularly in regards to programming and content. Still, even those beginnings had a bit of a political agenda attached to them, and that agenda was to steer Canadians toward their own culture and identity in the face of the growing attention

141

being paid to the many broadcasters in the United States. Canadian content guidelines were set in place, and networks were established in the official languages of French and English.

Television arrived twenty years later, in the early 1950s, adding a face to the voice, and brought both pleasures and problems. (Some say the fabulous original CBC/Radio-Canada logo with its wings flanking the upper half of the continent was first shown on TV either upside down or sideways.) I would, however, likely not be alone were I to say that when I think of the CBC, it is most often as a disembodied voice, a whisper, or sometimes a shout in my ear. And then there's the music. In other words, I think of radio.

Until the big and not very attractive building boom of the last several decades, CBC Radio was broadcast from a number of wonderfully eclectic locations. On Jarvis Street in Toronto, in the former home of Havergal College, a girls' private school (it moved to more upscale digs), the flagship CBC lived and thrived inside a rabbit warren of corridors and studios, all floored with battleship linoleum. Standing alongside this intriguing building was its lattice tower, which was, for half a decade or so, the tallest structure in the city. What an array of sounds were sent out from that tower: declarations of war, speeches by Winston Churchill, agricultural news and advice, symphony orchestras, hockey victories and humiliations, and brilliant, seminal literary programs such as Bob Weaver's *Anthology*.

The castle-like CPR and CNR hotels figured in all this dissemination of Canadian information, making those fortresses even more magical and multi-faceted than they already were. For eighty years, the French and English versions of the Ottawa CBC were broadcast from the eighth floor of the magnificent Château Laurier, a building that focuses the attention as much as any of the neighbouring architecture on nearby Parliament Hill. In British Columbia, the mezzanine floor of the Hotel Vancouver housed news and information studios, while on the ground floor, in art deco surroundings, radio drama and orchestral numbers were enacted. To add to the glamour, a weekly show called *The Roof*, featuring Dal Richards, his eleven-piece band, and a singer called Juliette, was beamed across the country from the ballroom on the top floor.

That ballroom would have been pictured in the imaginations of people all over the country: the farmer housebound by winter in the Prairies; miners in Northern Ontario; fishermen in Nova Scotia; women who never had seen, and never would see, a ballroom; men waiting to go to war; veterans returned from the war. And it would especially shine in the minds of children who, like me, listened in their darkened bedrooms after lights out from coast to coast to coast. The

music and the voices were adult and faint and very far away. The room our imaginations built was gilded and frescoed and festooned with chandeliers. The men and women dancing there were young and beautiful and under the spell of the most perfect kind of romantic love.

The imperfections of an actual ballroom would never be able to compete.

Robe

I N 1951, THE MASSEY COMMISSION (FORMALLY known as the Royal Commission on National Development in the Arts, Letters, and Sciences) released its report on the state of Canadian culture. Canada, so young a nation and still a colonial society in so many ways, wanted its own voice and vision in the arts—an arena that until that moment had mostly been dominated by Britain, and one that was beginning to be dominated by the United States. The commission, chaired by a former governor general, Vincent Massey, made several recommendations that directly or indirectly gave birth to many important cultural organizations—the National Library, the Canada Council for the Arts, and CBC Television among them. Those who came of age in the arts during the thrilling developmental period of the second half of Canada's twentieth century were the beneficiaries of these exciting programs. Artists, writers, musicians, actors, dancers, and filmmakers were encouraged and embraced. Suddenly almost anything seemed possible.

By 1953, when the brand-new Stratford Shakespearean Festival decided to launch its first lineup in a large tent assembled in a park in Stratford, Ontario, the sense of optimism engendered by the Massey Commission was very much in the air. After the Second World War, and possibly because of it, Canada had entered a period of economic and political stability. The manufacturing sector in many places was flourishing, and the Liberal Party, first under Mackenzie King and then under Louis St-Laurent, had achieved four consecutive majority governments, and was about to be elected for a fifth. The energy that attaches itself to a collective interest in the arts was palpable in cities across the country. But it was also evident in the town of Stratford, where the railway industry had cooled but the cultural industry was about to heat up.

Born in Stratford, journalist Tom Patterson felt the moment was right to establish a Shakespearean festival that would live up to the town's famous name. Astonishingly, he was able not only to convince the town council to back the idea, but also to hire the celebrated British stage director Tyrone Guthrie to oversee the first season. Soon the renowned actor Alec Guinness had agreed to star in *Richard III*, and the brilliant theatre designer Tanya Moiseiwitsch got to work on costumes such as this splendid robe, as well as the plans for the thrust stage where the hunchbacked king would play out his destiny.

During that same inaugural summer of 1953, in Northumberland County, another extraordinary decision was taken, and those of us who were small children at the time watched in amazement as five of our mothers and our aunts put on high-heeled shoes and their Sunday best, stepped into a car, and vanished, leaving us alone overnight with our fathers. They had said they were going to drive the two hundred miles to Stratford to see Alec Guinness play Richard III, and they had evidently meant it. The fact that a director of Tyrone Guthrie's stature and an actor as gifted and famous as Alec Guinness had come to Canada to participate in a Shakespearean festival in rural Ontario was something these women could not have even imagined during their childhoods. Now that it had miraculously occurred in their adulthoods, they were bound and determined not to miss it.

The journey would have been a bucolic treat in those days before freeways fully entered our world. My mother and my aunts would have driven in the shade of the maples of full summer, past fields lush with grain, and down the main streets of royalist Ontario towns named after English battles and princes: Cobourg, Agincourt, Georgetown, Waterloo. And then, in the evening, the duke himself—duplicitous, paranoid, plotting to become king. "I am determined to

prove a villain," he announces. "And hate the idle pleasures of these days."

How awe-inspiring it must have been to be members of that audience! To see Guinness perform, yes, but also to be a witness to all the young Canadians—many of whom would become our biggest stars—who played alongside as part of the company. There was no question, now, that Canada was blossoming and would continue to blossom culturally in the years to come. My mother and my aunts were still electric with enthusiasm when they returned to their daily domestic lives, and they passed on to their husbands and children an appetite for the arts, a desire to participate, and a fuller understanding of Canada's cultural worth.

Glasses

To MANY CANADIANS OF A CERTAIN AGE, Tommy Douglas looked exactly like what someone from the province of Saskatchewan should look like: slim as a stalk of wheat, muscular as a Clydesdale, pure as a Prairie sky, and wearing the kind of practical glasses that imply a clarity and breadth of vision striking in its farsightedness. And yet, in spite of the suggestion that Prairie life was in his DNA, Douglas was a transplant. He was the son of a Scottish ironmonger who packed up his family and moved to the Canadian central plains when Tommy was seven. He arrived in Winnipeg just in time for his son to witness the 1919 Winnipeg General Strike. The violence and the police brutality associated with those dark days would be something Tommy never forgot.

Tommy was drawn to public life, not for reasons of power or celebrity, but rather because, as a socialist, a Baptist min-

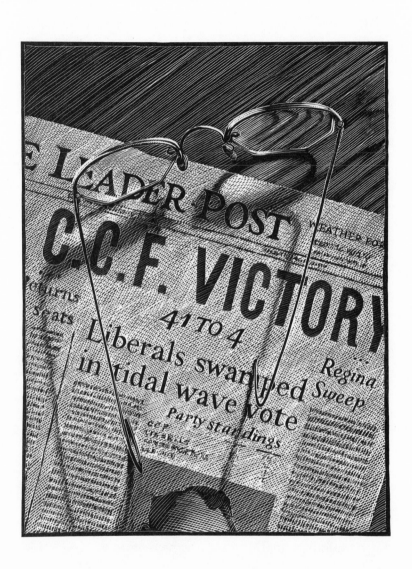

ister, and a deeply spiritual man, he believed that politics in the right hands could be used as a tool to promote moral and social change. As a representative of the Co-operative Commonwealth Federation (CCF) and later as head of the NDP, he would never become prime minister. And yet the important measures passed during Tommy Douglas's tenure in Parliament related more to his vision—and his magical ability to cause colleagues from all parties to pay respectful attention to that vision—than they did to raw political power. His focus was simple: he wanted to see programs put in place that would benefit all Canadians, all the time. He believed that a fair and just society was more than possible; it was essential.

Douglas was a firm promoter and defender of the Canada Pension Plan, which came into being under the government of Lester B. Pearson in 1966. But it was as the CCF premier of Saskatchewan that he really made his mark, by establishing a province-wide universal healthcare system, thereby providing a template for the national medicare program that would eventually come into being. To many, both in our country and beyond its borders, Canada's medicare program is a great part of what defines us and makes us a humane society. As Douglas himself said in a 1958 speech to Saskatchewan voters:

If we can do this—then I would like to hazard a prophecy that, before 1970, almost every other province in

*Canada will have followed the lead of Saskatchewan,
and we shall have a national health insurance program from the Atlantic to the Pacific.*

By the time Douglas died in 1986, all that he'd predicted had
come to pass, and in 2004, as the Father of Medicare, he was
voted the greatest Canadian of all time by viewers and listen-
ers of the Canadian Broadcasting Corporation.

Turban

BY THE TIME NELSON EDDY WAS YODELLING around the Rocky Mountains with Jeanette Mac-Donald in the 1936 black-and-white film called *Rose Marie*, the Royal Canadian Mounted Police, or Mounties, had gained worldwide iconic status. This was at least partly due to the unique appearance of the men when they were wearing their Red Serge, or dress uniform, a look so bewitching it can be recognized almost anywhere. The uniform comprises a scarlet jacket, blue jodhpurs (with a yellow stripe), brown leather boots, belt and side-strap, and on all but the coldest days, when a fur cap known as a busby is donned, a wide-brimmed, peaked Stetson hat—sometimes referred to as a campaign hat—similar to ones seen on the heads of boy scouts, park rangers, and Smokey the Bear.

During the nineteenth century, when the force was still known as the North-West Mounted Police (it did not receive its "Royal" status until 1904), the headgear of choice was a British pith helmet, pure white in colour. The fact that this surprising piece of information is so difficult for our imaginations to visualize goes a long way toward demonstrating just how compelling—and entrenched—the Mountie image has become over the years. You would think that the RCMP itself invented scarlet tunics, Sam Browne belts, and that pale brown wide-brimmed hat with the un-Canadian dip known as a Montana crease in its peaked centre. This was especially true in relation to the discussion that ensued when, in 1988, Baltej Singh Dhillon, who met all the criteria for becoming an RCMP recruit, was denied entry into the force because, as part of his Sikh religion, he maintained a beard (members of the force are normally clean-shaven) and wore a turban.

Dhillon, who had studied criminology after graduating from high school, appealed the decision, and in April 1989, the RCMP commissioner recommended that the prohibition against turbans be withdrawn.

Sikhs have been citizens of Canada since the nineteenth century. They have been pioneers, farmers, labourers, scholars, and every kind of professional one can imagine. Their religion dictates that those who are believers must also be warriors in the cause of upholding equality, truth, and justice, and—perhaps partly as a result of this—Sikhs have always been celebrated as excellent soldiers and police officers. Turban-wearing Sikh soldiers from India were famous

for their horsemanship, skill, and bravery in the First World War, and in fact, almost a dozen Sikhs from the Dominion of Canada fought alongside their fellow Canadians in that conflict.

Sadly, little of this was recalled after the RCMP commissioner's recommendation that Sikh officers should be permitted to wear their turbans when in uniform. The debate was heated: anti-turban petitions were circulated, and deprecating pins were worn. Some Canadians objected on the grounds of safety, insisting that the turban made Sikh officers an easy target, or (my favourite) that murderers would be able to strangle them with the cloth from their own turbans.

In the end, however, the Charter of Rights and Freedoms was consulted, justice prevailed, and Baltej Singh Dhillon was able to honour both his vocation and his religion. As Solicitor General Pierre Cadieux said in Parliament in March 1990, the change "squared with Canadian human rights legislation," and reflected the government's "strong commitment to a multicultural society."

To my mind, the inclusion of the Sikh turban has added an elegant and meaningful variation to a uniform in danger of becoming the kind of kitschy stereotype we have seen in cartoons and Monty Python skits. A turban in conjunction with the Red Serge is a beautiful sight to behold.

Twenty-five years later, another Sikh who has worn a uniform and a turban has come to public attention.

Harjit Singh Sajjan served as a lieutenant-colonel with the Canadian Armed Forces, with tours in Bosnia and Afghanistan, and was for eleven years a member of the Vancouver Police Department. In November 2015, after being elected as the MP for Vancouver South in British Columbia, he was appointed minister of national defence in Justin Trudeau's newly elected Liberal government.

Machine

FOUNDED IN 1870 AND NAMED AFTER WILLIAM McMurray, a Hudson's Bay Company factor, Fort McMurray and the surrounding territory has drawn attention to Canada over the years for varying reasons. It was from nearby Fort Chipewyan, on Lake Athabasca, that, in 1789, Alexander Mackenzie famously set out to attempt to find a passage to the West Coast. With the help of a Chipewyan guide and advisers from several West Coast tribes, he was ultimately successful in this endeavour in 1793. But on this 1789 voyage, he passed by, and made the first recorded comment concerning, the Athabasca tar sands.

Fort McMurray would be established more than half a century later at the confluence of the Athabasca and Clearwater Rivers, and it became well known for the wealth of furs brought by First Nations and Métis hunters to the site. The hunters also brought information concerning the vast amount of tar present in Lake Athabasca and in the Athabasca River—tar that was helpful when waterproofing or mending a canoe, but that was also sometimes so thick and plentiful it was impossible to disembark in its midst.

Men like Mackenzie—and indeed McMurray himself—were fascinating, complex, and often brilliant individuals whose skills included the ability to travel over vast tracts of wilderness landscape in furious weather, to speak a number of First Nations languages, and to record the specifics of the natural environment through which they passed. They are often referred to, romantically, as adventurers or explorers, but the current that underlay their various quests had its source in something a good deal more prosaic: commerce. The bitter rivalry that existed in the fur trade between the Hudson's Bay Company and the North West Company would play itself out in this northwestern part of what would become Alberta when, in 1821, the two companies merged under one name—the Hudson's Bay Company. The seemingly insatiable desire for fur, and the massive corporate gains that came from it, continued unabated for another hundred years. After that, the company opened a number of successful department stores and even ventured into the developing oil and gas industry.

I hardly need say that northwestern Alberta is now infinitely less known for its connection to the fur trade than it is for its association with a vast oil and gas industry born as the result of refining the same tar talked about by First Nations traders two hundred years ago. This tar sands enterprise has been both celebrated for its economic success—until the recent collapse in oil prices—and reviled for its increasingly negative impact on the environment. There have been social consequences as well: First Nations stakeholders have concerns about the pollution of their traditional fishing and hunting grounds; Canada's environmental reputation has been questioned internationally; and a whole generation of young men, mostly from the Maritime Provinces, where after the collapse of the fisheries unemployment rates were high, have been displaced in order to work as labourers for Suncor or Syncrude.

Approximately one thousand of those labourers drive gigantic trucks the size of a three-storey house. Vehicles such as these manoeuvre on massive tires that cost over fifty thousand dollars each. Great numbers of other workers operate enormous shovels that can lift over a half ton of material in one scoop, and that burn upward of two thousand gallons of diesel in the course of a single shift. Before this equipment can be used to haul the oil-rich sands to a refinery, it must remove the "overburden" of trees, soil, rocks, wetlands, small lakes, streams—in other words, the details of the landscape, the natural world as we know it.

One wonders how the town's namesake, William McMurray, would have viewed this. He was a man who

thought nothing of walking for days in bone-chilling temperatures to attend a New Year's party at Fort Chipewyan, and who was said to be one of the best orators in the Salteaux and Chipewyan languages. It was a different time. And he himself was a key player in a large corporation bent on exploiting the natural resources of the area. The impact of the fur trade on the animal population of the West was immeasurable and irredeemable. And European contact at its best changed forever and at its worst completely destroyed First Nations tribes. Still, regardless of the damage he and men like him were responsible for, had William McMurray looked at the environmental impact of the tar sands, which is so extensive it can be seen from outer space, I think even he might have turned to us and beseeched us to find another way.

Bush Plane

I T IS QUITE POSSIBLE THAT AFTER I WAS BORN, one of the first mechanical sounds that entered my ears was made by the arrival of a bush plane on Kenogamisis Lake, the shore of which lay just beyond the windows of the small company hospital where my mother gave birth. Because it was June, I might also have heard the splash of pontoons as they touched the water. The little aviation hangar was nearby, which explained the frequent appearance of aircraft on floats (or in the winter, on skis).

The North as my mother and father knew it might never have been settled had it not been for bush planes that delivered explorers, prospectors, and speculators—and in their wake, bankers, lawyers, nurses, doctors, and shopkeepers. After that, they transported a variety of merchandise and supplies, performed rescue missions, brought the news, dropped off piano examination adjudicators and travelling

performers, acted as water bombers during forest fires, mapped the terrain with the help of "belly cameras," and brought the mail. My mother, who began to subscribe in the late 1930s, received her first copies of *The New Yorker* in this way, as well as her Book of the Month Club pick.

The plane I might have heard could have been a Fairchild or a Norseman, both dependable servants in opening and supplying Canada's northland. Or it could have been a de Havilland Beaver, the bush plane that was, and continues to be, the darling of the pilots of the North. During those first years of my life, the de Havilland Beaver would have been a recurrent visitor, as it was the aircraft of choice for the Ontario Department of Lands and Forests and busily hopped, therefore, from lake to lake all over the North.

The first flight that I remember taking was in a Beaver when I was about four, and as a result of it, I can recall the exact moment when I became aware of the distance between me and the ground. I had thought, after takeoff, that the little log houses lined up along the lake were toys, but as they became smaller and smaller, my depth perception kicked in in a frighteningly vivid way. That faraway world showed itself to be unreliable, tilting, distant, and then gone from my view.

I thought it might have been a de Havilland Beaver that flew my family even farther north a few years before, in 1950, to Ossu Lake (Ossu was short for O'Sullivan), where my father was hoping a mine would develop. But my older brother Nick assures me it was a Norseman that conveyed us to the lake-side cabin where we were to spend the summer. The chief of the local Anishinaabe tribe paddled across the lake to greet us, I was told, and brought with him his three little girls for me to play with and a small pair of embroidered deerskin moccasins for me to wear. Such courtesy and generosity in the face of our noisy mechanical entry and the potential for utter change that might have followed in our wake!

The plans for the Lake Ossu mine were ultimately abandoned, however. Decades later, my brother Nick found the remains of the modest log cabin where our family had spent that summer of 1951. It and the few other log outbuildings around it were being taken back by the bush. The little moccasins, on the other hand, have remained forever among my prized possessions.

Prayer Mat

BY 1957, MY FAMILY AND I HAD SETTLED INTO a red-brick house on Chudleigh Avenue in the small colonial city of Toronto, Ontario. North of Lake Superior, Little Long Lac Gold Mine had almost fully closed, but my father, who was doing contract prospecting for city speculators on Bay Street, still regularly flew north from the Toronto Island Airport. I was going to a red-brick city school with large windows and a cinder playground where I was taught about the kings and queens of England, the explorers, and how to draw and colour the Union Jack, flag of the Empire. I thought this flag was the most beautiful thing I had ever seen and was almost as proud of these drawings as I was of the cardboard diorama of Magellan that I made in art class. I presented him meeting his end in the South Seas—full of arrows and bloodying the turquoise waters that fronted a lush tropical paradise full of palm trees, the branches of which I had painstakingly painted in an unlikely emerald green.

School activities such as these were thrilling for me. But because I was the much younger child in the family, weekends were very quiet. Still, there was the highlight of Sundays at St. Simon's Anglican Church, where the stained-glass windows were mesmerizing, and where my older brother sang in the celebrated all-male choir. Near our summer place in rural Ontario there was an Anglican church as well, and I was sometimes taken there on Sundays. It had been built in 1840 out of wood the pioneers had harvested from the nearby virgin forests. The impressive steeple surmounted two doors that made a Gothic arch when they were closed. It was lovely in a simple, almost Quaker, and certainly North American way, while the architecture of St. Simon's in the city attempted to reproduce, albeit in a smaller manner, the demeanour of its English cousins overseas.

While I attended St. Simon's in the winter and the rural Ontario church in the summer of 1957, Rajjab Assim, an Albanian-born Muslim, was responding to the increasing internationalization of Toronto's Muslim community by changing the name of the Albanian Muslim Society to the more inclusive Muslim Society of Toronto. And soon thereafter, the first Toronto mosque opened in a storefront at 3047 Dundas Street West. The society rented the building for a few years, and then purchased it in 1961. Eventually, as

the community grew, the decision to sell the building was taken, and a larger space was purchased. But this was not the end of the story of Toronto's storefront mosques, which have continued to flourish in the city until the present day.

In 2012, I was interviewed by CBC's *Ontario Today* on the subject of "bricks and mortar"—whether beautiful architecture is needed to access the spiritual. I was concerned about the imminent closure of the rural Anglican church I had known as a child: it was important to my family, and it was one that I, and others, considered to be of great historical and architectural significance, as well as physically beautiful. *Ontario Today* also interviewed Himy Syed, a businessman, blogger, aspiring politician, and devout Muslim. He spoke of one storefront mosque, Al-Qalam Islamic Community Centre (a leased space that was part of a strip mall). Many community events, the evening Islamic school, and sessions of prayer took place within its walls, he told us. When asked about beauty and the spiritual, he made reference to prayer mats, how they could be taken into any clean space for prayer, and how they were both visually pleasing and symbolically profound in their design. Niches at the top were to be pointed toward Mecca, for example, and often lamps were included, referencing the verse of light, one of the most important and beautiful passages in the Quran. "You may have the simplest room where people will pray," he said. "It may be a hallway, a temporary basement, a parking garage underneath a building, an office tower. And you will find the most beautiful prayer mat."

I thought of the men and women—small-business owners, farmers, and aspiring politicians—founding the pioneer Anglican church that I was now trying to save. They would all have been recent arrivals in this new land in the 1840s, and they would have needed somewhere to gather, meditate, pray, and enjoy fellowship. What they built would have been quite basic in the beginning—the stained glass came later—and would have accrued power and beauty with age, so that by the time I looked at it, it seemed like a rare gem. I thought about how this need for community and sanctity is something we all share, regardless of where it is housed. A storefront in a strip mall can be a home for prayer, education, and friendship, as can a rough post-and-beam, community-built wooden structure situated in a small clearing in the wilderness. In a significant way, they are both small clearings in the wilderness, places where the light can enter.

Cree Basket

WANUSKEWIN IS AN ANCIENT SPIRITUAL site on the northern Great Plains, three miles north of the city of Saskatoon. Various First Nations tribes have gathered here for millennia, and archaeological evidence of human activity has been traced back to 4000 BCE. Since its official opening in 1992, the six-hundred-acre heritage site, controlled and operated by First Nations Plains peoples, has essentially been a museum about the landscape, located *in* and *on* the landscape. One of the last of a dozen prairie boulder medicine wheels is still intact here, and the sense of ceremony surrounding it is palpable. The flora and fauna, the dips and hollows of the landscape, the effect of wind on the earth and sky insist that the sanctity of all human experience be recognized. To visit this place—even for a few hours—is to be forever haunted by it.

I myself was fortunate enough to be taken to Wanuskewin

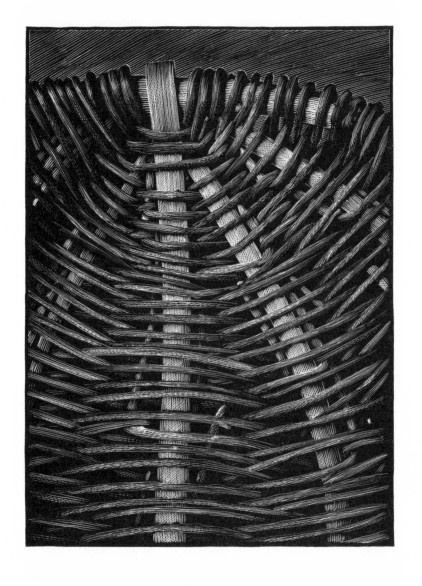

in the summer of 1993 by Cree poet Louise Halfe. Some of her grandmothers were making things on the land, she informed me, and we should go out to see them. I had known Louise long enough to understand that when she spoke about her grandmothers, she could be referring to any older women in the Cree community, not just those to whom she was directly related by blood. But sometimes the grandmothers she referred to *were* her ancestors, and those were the ones she often spoke to—and with—when she was writing poetry.

It was a clear and bright Prairie day, clouds hurrying overhead, and the sense of the South Saskatchewan River nearby. Prairie grasses bent in the wind and the grandmothers were indeed there, making baskets. We chatted with them for a while, then asked if one of them would take our picture near a large boulder of the medicine wheel. Later I would paste that picture into an album I kept at the time, which is still on a shelf near the desk where I write.

The basket I took back to Ontario from Wanuskewin has been with me ever since that day. It has moved from home to home when I have moved, and has been present at the meals of family and friends. Every time I look at it, I remember the wise, kind face of the grandmother who made it. And I remember Louise and me, how much younger we were, and how Louise placed some tobacco under a boulder as an offering to the land.

In 2005, Louise Halfe, also known as Sky Dancer, was named poet laureate of Saskatchewan.

Lighthouse

I N SPITE OF THE DIFFICULTIES INVOLVED IN THE measurement of something as elusive as the place where the water meets the land, it is safe to say that Canada has by far the longest coastline in the world, and by extension, the greatest need for lighthouses. A lot of hope and trust and democratic thought went into the construction of the numerous lighthouses that arose from this need; protection from harm and comfort during storms for all sailors are two of their most important reasons for being. My sense is that lighthouses were never meant to be as beautiful as they are, but that form followed function, and perhaps because the function involved was so noble, all lighthouses seem perfectly designed for their place in the landscape. There are few among us who would pass up an opportunity to venture out to the lighthouse on a summer afternoon. We are quite simply drawn to them.

The first lighthouse in Canada was built across the bay from the French Fortress of Louisbourg in 1734, in what is now Cape Breton. Octagonal in shape and almost seventy feet high, the lighthouse had a lantern made of four hundred small panes surrounding a circle of thirty-two oil-fed wicks enhanced by polished metal refractors. Apparently, it could be seen for up to twelve nautical miles—a great achievement for its day—but the heat from all those flames was too intense, and in time the lantern self-destructed. It was replaced by a lantern with fewer wicks that was cooled by a jacket of water. This version of the lamp survived until the final, and very successful, sacking of Louisbourg by the English in 1758.

The intermediate lighthouse at Louisbourg was made of wood and built by the English almost a hundred years later, in 1848, and after it burned in 1923, the current tower was erected. Although it too is octagonal, it is not quite as tall as its grandfather. Nevertheless, its proportions are absolutely suited to the shapes of the rocks surrounding it, and it marks—and somehow dignifies—this one exposed part of the coast of Nova Scotia.

I sometimes think about the duties connected to the now almost completely extinct profession of lighthouse keeper. They were required to keep the light, of course, by trimming wicks, replacing fuel, and polishing glass, and they had to maintain the signals and radio communications, as well as the fog alarm. They also performed acts of rescue and provided sanctuary. Here in Canada, they would often have been the only human heart beating in a vast, empty terrain fronted by ferocious and seemingly endless waters. They and their towers speak to the better, more charitable side of human nature. Although far too many of them have disappeared, I cannot stop believing that all the Canadian lighthouses are still there, standing like sentinels on our islands and headlands, cutting through the dark, wild storm, holding out long arms of light to gather us all—from sea to sea to sea—into a safe harbour.

Mace

O N A BITTERLY COLD NIGHT IN FEBRUARY 1916, the inhabitants of Ottawa, Ontario, were amazed to see the sky behind the Houses of Parliament turn orange as flames emerged from the windows and roof of the Centre Block. Aided by the building's ventilation system, the conflagration moved at a swift pace, devouring all wood and paper it came in contact with. The Library of Parliament, which was not a separate building at the time, would have been engulfed as well had it not been for two metal fire doors that the parliamentary librarian had the presence of mind to close. Seven people were killed in this catastrophe, including one MP and two visitors to the Speaker's quarters, where the fire was particularly intense.

By the next morning, the building where the House of Commons normally convened had been transformed into an ominous-looking ice palace darkened here and there by soot.

Twisted metal and charred timbers lay in contorted positions around the foundation, and the old clock from the central tower, which purportedly had continued to tick and chime until the tower fell, was smashed on the ground. Rescued furniture and relics were piled haphazardly in the snow, and in some cases were covered in ice themselves. But one thing that was neither rescued nor hosed down and then frozen was the mace. And this was a big problem for Parliament.

A mace is a large, decorated club-like accoutrement, normally made of precious metals and sometimes encrusted with jewels, which is carried in front of the Speaker of the House by the sergeant-at-arms as they make their entry into the House of Commons. It is meant to symbolize the authority of Parliament (and sovereign approval), and as such it has great power. It would be out of order for Parliament to function without it. Many of the former colonies of the British Empire—Canada among them—still maintain the tradition of having the mace present whenever Parliament is in session.

Over the years, likely because of their symbolic and actual heftiness, maces have played a role in the kind of bun-throwing arguments that sometimes break out during Question Period in various Commonwealth Houses of Commons. Maces have been banged on tables, pushed off their cushions and onto the floor, seized and carried off, and wrestled over. Once, in 1965 in the Bahamas, an MP was so enraged by gerrymandering on the part of an opposing party,

he grabbed the mace and threw it out the window, where it broke into pieces on the lawn. When such things happen, not only is the member who engaged in the activity dismissed from the House, at least for a period of time, but the House itself is dismissed until a suitable replacement mace can be found. Luckily for the Bahamians, Canada had just such a replacement mace available for loan.

In February 1916, two or three days after the fire, the original and unrescued Canadian mace was found in the wreckage of the Speaker's quarters. All its gold and silver ornamentation, its royal seal and parliamentary authority had been reduced to a conglomerate no larger than a tennis ball. Under these circumstances, the House could not meet even to discuss how to clean up after the catastrophe. So the Senate, whose mace *had* been rescued, offered theirs as an interim solution while a wooden replacement mace was carved and gilded in a local workshop. The wooden mace was used until the city of London, England, donated another gold-and-silver mace in which was incorporated the conglomerate of the first.

When the Bahamians were in need, therefore, the Canadian replacement mace from 1916 was pressed into service. It was returned, freshly gilded, once the Bahamians had installed a new mace. In Canada, the wooden mace is used in the House only once a year—on the anniversary of the 1916 fire.

184

Admittedly, all this has certain Lewis Carroll/Mad Hatter overtones. Still, the mace itself is a beautiful object, and a fine example of the work of a gifted silversmith. The pomp and ceremony with which it is treated pays tribute to the past. And the democratic values it symbolizes, those of a representational government, are worth both honouring and protecting.

Codfish

WHEN, AS THE VERY FIRST "COME FROM away" writer-in-residence, I arrived in St. John's, Newfoundland, in the autumn of 1992, I was entering that fascinating and unique culture at a significant time. I had visited Newfoundland once before, on a reading tour, and had fallen in love with the multicoloured houses on streets that somersault down to the harbour, the song in the speech of the inhabitants, the warmth and energy of the people, the freshly caught codfish that could be bought on the docks. From the minute I stepped in a cab at the airport and the driver launched into a story about his grandfather—who was a "hard case" and had, at ninety-six years of age, been arrested in a bar brawl the previous evening—I knew I was no longer in Kansas. While the cabby continued his tale in an ancient Irish accent, we were passing by some of the most elegant and historic wooden architecture in North America. At the bottom of each street, the inky waters of one of the most spectacular natural harbours in the world bristled in the breeze, and I could see brightly painted fishing vessels moored at the docks. If this place didn't exist, I might have had to invent it, I thought. This notion became a certainty as the days passed by.

Mary Dalton, the brilliant St. John's poet and scholar who had invited me to this magical place, took me down to the harbour and then back to her ship-like kitchen, where she cooked fish while I looked out her windows at the geometry of painted clapboard and upright wooden fence boards. Everything was fresh—the air; the codfish we ate; the ideas Mary expressed about poetry; her clear, thoughtful expression; the noisy, laughter-filled party she took me to after my reading. There was no question about it: I knew I had to come back. A year later, I did not hesitate for a moment when the invitation to be writer-in-residence arrived at my door.

In the course of the intervening year, however, there had been a seismic change in Newfoundland. Just two months in advance of my second arrival in 1992, Fisheries Minister John Crosbie had made a shocking announcement: the codfish stocks were down to 1 percent of their 1958 volume, meaning that the fish itself was to all intents and purposes extinct. On government orders, he told a crowd of angry fishermen in Bay Bulls that there would be a moratorium on fishing for cod for the next two years—and perhaps longer. He was right

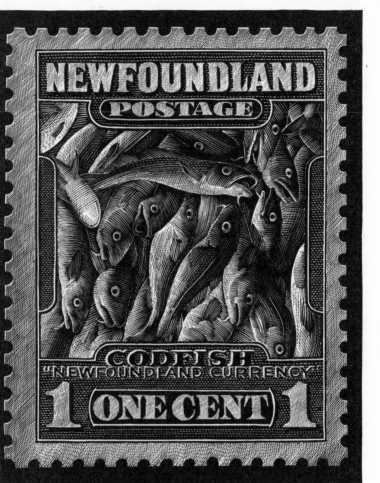

about "longer." The moratorium, which instantly put thirty thousand people out of work (the largest layoff in Canadian history), has lasted until the present day, and in spite of some signs that cod stocks are recovering, no one knows how much longer the ban will be in effect.

What led up to this catastrophe was a tangled web of federal government mismanagement, global greed, ignorance, and a sometimes wilful and complete lack of care. Inshore small fishermen, who by their very nature were unable to do anything except fish sustainably, had been telling the government for decades that the fish stocks were lowering by significant amounts each year, and that foreign trawlers were taking the complete catch out on the nose and the tail of the famous Grand Banks. European companies in particular (though there were other nations as well) were using floating fish factories and dragnets to hoover up absolutely everything from the ocean floor, then freezing their gigantic catches on the spot.

The cod fishery has greatly contributed to the culture, survival, livelihood, and architecture of Newfoundland and Labrador for over four hundred years. On an island where originality of language is important to sense of place and unmistakable on the human tongue and in the written word, there are hundreds of terms in J. Widdowson, W.J. Kirwin, and George Story's wonderful *Dictionary of Newfoundland English* that relate not only to the fishery in general but to the cod fishery in particular. Even those of us who have never seen salt water know that Newfoundland without its fishermen and its fishery is a diminished Newfoundland. The problem was that no one in power respected those fishermen enough to listen to what they were trying to tell us.

It is important to note that the 1932 stamp pictured here was in circulation seventeen years before Newfoundland became Canada's tenth province. Although a local journalist of the time, Albert Perlin, called it "the ugliest stamp ever issued"—an opinion I do not share, by the way—it accurately represents the central role, and the amplitude, of a codfish catch in Newfoundland.

There are some who believe that the decline in the cod stocks began with Confederation in 1949 and the federal government's inability, or unwillingness, to deal with the might of foreign multinational fishing corporations. There is, of course, no way to fully prove this. But thirty years after Confederation, and a dozen years before the death of the cod industry, Canadian folksinger Stan Rogers wrote a song about the Atlantic fishery that indicated at least *he* had been listening to the fishermen. The lyrics of "Make and Break Harbour" powerfully depict the sadness of a disappearing way of life, and bring back to mind the pain on the faces of those people in Bay Bulls in 1992, when John Crosbie gave them the news:

In Make and Break Harbour the boats are so few.
Too many are pulled up and rotten.
Most houses stand empty. Old nets hung to dry
Are blown away, lost and forgotten.

More than two decades after the moratorium was put in place, there are now reports that indicate the cod stocks may be rising. Whether we shall ever see the wealth of cod that thrived in earlier waters remains unclear. But the people who fished and the places they sailed from cannot be reassembled in anything like the way we remember them, though the music and legends of their culture will always be kept alive.

Violin

LIKE SO MANY OF US IN CANADA, THIS VIOLIN, made in 1782 by the celebrated luthier G.B. Guadagnini during his important Turin period, is an immigrant—one that, in the hands and heart of another immigrant, Jacques Israelievitch, delighted many Canadian music lovers for over a quarter of a century.

Israelievitch was most certainly a prodigy, and with the exception of a few mean-spirited anti-Semitic taunts in the playground, he had a happy and very productive French childhood. Born in Cannes, he began his musical education in Le Mans, becoming the youngest student ever to graduate from the Le Mans Conservatoire. He made his first appearance on French national radio when he was just eleven, and after studying with Henryk Szeryng and René Benedetti at the Conservatoire de Paris, he graduated from that school when he was only sixteen.

It was then that, sponsored by the Baroness de Rothschild, he came to North America to study at Indiana University with such brilliant musicians as Josef Gingold and János Starker. Then, in 1972, at the age of twenty-three, this very young man was appointed assistant concertmaster of the Chicago Symphony Orchestra, where the renowned Sir Georg Solti was conductor. Six years later, Israelievitch was named concertmaster of the St. Louis Symphony Orchestra, a position he would hold for ten years.

By the time that decade was over, Jacques Israelievitch had met and fallen in love with the two great loves of his life: his wife, Gabrielle, and the Guadagnini violin. The mortgage for the latter was paid off by an anonymous patron as a wedding gift when he married the former, so in a sense, it could be said that Israelievitch married the Guadagnini and Gabrielle at the same time. (The anonymous patron and her son were soon identified and became close friends of the Israelievitches.)

In 1988, Günther Herbig invited Israelievitch to become the concertmaster of the Toronto Symphony Orchestra, and Jacques, his family, and the 1782 Guadagnini immigrated to Canada, where Jacques would become a citizen and remain for the rest of his life, playing with the TSO and chamber music groups, recording, and teaching master classes to students who adored him. The Guadagnini violin was rarely out of his arms, but another courtship was under way, as

Jacques—and by extension, the Guadagnini—had fallen in love with a Peccatte bow that was a cherished part of a collection kept by Ric Heinl, third generation at the legendary George Heinl and Company (specialists in repairs and restoration of fine instruments) on Church Street in Toronto. No amount of pleading on Jacques's part, and no amount of mournful sighing on the part of the Guadagnini, could convince Ric to let the bow leave his collection, until Gabrielle successfully extracted it on the occasion of a significant anniversary of her marriage to Jacques.

When Jacques became ill, the Guadagnini violin and the Peccatte bow were always by his side, and often they were in his arms and in his hands. Astonishingly, Israelievitch gave concerts and taught students right up until the last month of his life. Moreover, even though he had thought he might be too weak to complete the twenty-eight Mozart violin sonatas he was recording with pianist Christina Petrowska Quilico, he and Quilico and the Guadagnini violin and the Peccatte bow finished the last six just months before he died. Both musicians wept while they played.

Then the day came when Jacques could no longer sit up and could therefore no longer play, and he knew, to his unimaginable grief, that although he was only sixty-seven years old, he would be unable to touch the violin and the bow again.

But the Guadagnini and the Peccatte would continue to

touch each other. When Gabrielle asked Jacques if he wanted Kaddish to be played at his funeral, he said yes. And when she asked who should play it, Jacques named his favourite student, a young Muslim Canadian called Amir Safavi.

Since that sad occasion, often, when he has a recital or concert, Amir has borrowed the Guadagnini violin and the Peccatte bow from Ric Heinl's shop, where they are lovingly housed, and he will continue to do so into the future. Because, as Jacques knew, and as Gabrielle recently said to me, a fiddle needs to be played.

Mountain Spirits

THE COASTAL REGIONS OF THE PACIFIC NORTH-west comprise some of the most beautiful landscapes in the world. Softened by rain and mist, or brought to dazzling life by sun, the combination of water, sky, islands, and mountains creates a gentle world of practically unreal loveliness, one that soothes the mind at the same time that it stimulates the senses. With its soft weather, clear waters, and warm rocks, this is a benign and inviting wilderness, and is particularly so on the still-untamed west coast of Vancouver Island.

This coast, and the nearby tip of Washington State, is the traditional territory of the Nuu-chah-nulth peoples, an amalgam of several different family-related tribes. The name means "all along the mountains and the sea," and describes the part of the world that these peoples have inhabited for millennia. Likely related to the Inuit culture at some time in

the past, they were largely whale hunters. The benevolent climate of their ancestral hunting area and the easy availability of other species of fish, game, and wildlife made for a life where all forms of art could not only develop but flourish. Nuu-chah-nulth cultural ceremonies included dance, song, storytelling, and theatre. But it was in the creation of sculpture, painting, totems, and architecture that these peoples were—and remain—beyond exceptional. Put simply, as evidenced by their totem poles, painted longhouses, and vivid, powerful masks, they created some of the most important works of art in the world.

These Mountain Spirit masks, now in the Royal British Columbia Museum in Victoria, form an immediate relationship with the viewer. Their open mouths are singing the mountain landscape and breathing the mountain wind. Moreover, they seem themselves to be germinating, turning into landscape. Once the masks with their horizontal leafy headdresses were donned, it would have been possible to believe that vines and cedar boughs might emerge from the wearer's arms and feet, as he danced beneath a canopy of the magnificent trees that are still visible all along Vancouver Island's astonishing, spirit-filled west coast.

Old Walt

MY MATRILINEAL IRISH FOREBEARS OF THE
1840s settled near Norwood, Ontario, in Peter-
borough County, close enough to the rock of
the Canadian Shield that their land was difficult at best. But
being Irish, they were used to difficult land, and with hard
work, they were able to chop out enough pasture to support
some animals, and to build some outbuildings so that those
animals, and their feed, would survive the winter. By the early
1900s, the family had managed to move to better land farther
south in Northumberland County, though they never made
it down to the coveted soil nearer "the front" of Lake Ontario.
The work was still hard and the winters were still long, but
the family was gifted at producing over a half-dozen healthy
sons (they achieved this in more than one generation), and
that made things much more manageable.

After the First World War and into the early 1920s,

my grandfather and his brothers were busy training their boy children, some of them still very small, in the ways of Ontario farming. The landscape that surrounded these boys would get into their blood in one way or another, but not in a sentimental or spiritual way. They knew it was home, and thought of it as such, and they valued the work they put into it—farming in spring, summer, and fall, and logging in winter. They valued the tribal ideas about family that they had brought with them from Ireland as well, and certain political associations, including the belief that they should be involved in municipal politics.

While these boys learned how to push the plough and handle a two-man crosscut saw, and were educated and later attended political meetings in one-room schoolhouses, something very different was going on in neighbouring Hastings County in the landscape just twenty or twenty-five miles north of them. A left-leaning feminist and spiritualist named Flora MacDonald, and her husband, Howard Denison, had bought Bon Echo Inn on the edge of Mazinaw Lake—one of the most beautiful combinations of rock and waterscape in Ontario—where they intended to gather together as many painters and poets as they could. In that capacity, Flora's own son, Merrill Denison, and several of his friends would compose plays at the spot, and painters such as Frederic Marlett Bell-Smith, Arthur Lismer, and A.Y. Jackson would visit often. Some of them brought with them their absorption in theosophy, an esoteric religious philosophy that pondered the role of human life in a vast and unknowable universe.

Spirituality was not new to the location: the impressive Mazinaw Rock, much painted by the visiting artists of MacDonald's time, was covered in exceptional Ojibwa pictographs, mythical in subject matter and dating from long before European contact. Central to the painted motifs was the trickster figure Nanabush, who through surprise and originality engendered a creativity in the culture that caused events to unfold in a different and sometimes more life-enhancing way.

MacDonald had also founded an association of thinkers called the Whitmanites, who met at the lodge and celebrated American poet Walt Whitman's dedication to democracy, spirituality, and human rights. "My life's work from now on," she wrote about her hero, "will be propagating the ideals of Walt Whitman, with Bon Echo as a glorious vantage ground." Whitman, who had spent his entire life writing and rewriting, publishing and republishing his huge collection entitled *Leaves of Grass*, would be much read and thoroughly discussed by visitors to the lodge.

My great-uncles would have been utterly bewildered by all this attention to poetry and painting in an unfarmable, rocky landscape where they themselves could not have survived, and they would have wondered how on earth these folks kept body and soul together, or why they didn't make

an effort to move to better land. Chances are my uncles had never heard of Walt Whitman or *Leaves of Grass*, and would have been skeptical, if they had, of the fact that he was an American. They would have been mystified, therefore, had they heard that Flora MacDonald and American essayist Horace Traubel had commemorated the hundredth anniversary of Whitman's birth by having the lines

> *My foothold is tenon'd and mortised in granite*
> *I laugh at what you call dissolution*
> *And I know the amplitude of time*

carved into Mazinaw Rock's face under the heading "Old Walt." No, my uncles would not have understood the point of Walt Whitman.

But he understood the point of them, for Whitman was a lover of the working man. In section 94 of *Leaves of Grass*, "Carol of Occupations," Whitman conjures my uncles and their works:

> *In the labor of engines and trades, and the labor of fields,*
> *I find the developments,*
> *And find the eternal meanings.*

And in section 93, "A Farm Picture," his words show us the world they built:

204

Through the ample open door of the peaceful country
     barn,
A sunlit pasture field with cattle and horses feeding
And haze and vista, and the far horizon fading away.

The ancient Ojibwa with their ochre paintings of profound systems of belief, the large-hearted American poet who loved all humanity, my great-uncles, shaping the world with their labour, and the artists of the new country are all drawn together by the undeniable power and mystical spirit of this place.

Africville Church

ALL THROUGH LIFE THERE ARE MUCH-LOVED places that we leave behind, sometimes because we choose to and sometimes because we must. Rooms in which we have fallen in love, the distant silhouette of a town where we felt at home, beloved views—all this falls behind us as we walk forward, for life is full of change. But to be evicted from the place you and your antecedents knew as home, to know that the place has been destroyed, and that you can neither remain in it nor return to it, is a loss that is especially hard to bear.

Africville was an African Nova Scotian community that existed for over 110 years on the Halifax side of Bedford Basin. It was established in the 1840s, when a half-dozen men, originally from the community of Hammonds Plains, Nova Scotia, purchased land in this spot. African Nova Scotians had been living in Hammonds Plains ever since the American Revolution, but these young men wanted to be closer to Halifax in hopes of finding steady employment. As the years passed, children were born and the community that would become known as Africville developed and grew, and was passed from generation to generation.

A vibrant spiritual life developed around the first church, built in 1849. Many of the inhabitants of Africville were poor, but their focus on the family and the sense of fellowship connected to religion meant they measured quality of life differently. The Easter sunrise service, for instance, with its continuous and joyous singing and multiple baptisms in Bedford Basin, must have been a life-enhancing blessing to the human heart. When in 1916 the original church was replaced by the Seaview African United Baptist Church, services continued with equal fervour. Fifty years later, in the mid-1960s, this building was demolished by wrecking balls sent out by municipal employees whose elected bosses apparently favoured new development on the edges of Halifax, and who claimed that Africville had become a slum. At the same time, they sent machines to take down the homes of the sons and daughters of those who'd built the church.

It is impossible to compensate for the loss of a community, for the identity of such a place is organically, not artificially, developed. Still, this replica of the demolished church, in which the Africville Museum is housed, teaches us that

a different, but still strong, energy can rise from the ashes of that which is mistreated, undervalued, and ultimately erased. The replica of the Seaview African United Baptist Church does not make the eviction bearable, but it does enable us to imagine the singing at those many Easter sunrise services, and we ache to hear that joy.

Oyster

I HAVE ALWAYS THOUGHT THAT OYSTERS, SEA dwellers that they are, have shells that resemble small rocky islands of varying elevations, no two alike. Inside, of course, there is life and taste, a smooth opalescence, and sometimes treasure. But it is the outside—rough, ugly, and carbuncled—that gives them their character and their nobility. Opening and eating them carries with it the suggestion that we are disrupting and then swallowing a complete universe, one that has been protected by such a hard casing that our ability to prise out the moist centre seems like a miracle in itself. Few human beings will ever forget the surprise and delight of their first raw oyster. And in the end, the collection of discarded shells in the saucer is like either a contemporary art piece or a demolition site, depending on one's mood, point of view, and desire for more.

The Acadians were seventeenth-century French refugees

who settled in what would come to be known as Canada's Maritime Provinces. For over 150 years, they farmed the land and lived peacefully alongside the Mi'kmaq with whom they often intermarried. They also harvested oysters from the Bay of Fundy and other shallow coves and inlets in the vicinity. But at the end of a series of relentless and bewildering colonial wars, during which the French and the English jockeyed for dominance in North America, the British banished many of the Acadians from the marshes, coastlines, and valleys that had become their North American home. At the time of this Grand Dérangement, 11,500 French-speaking Acadians were sent to the southern colony of Louisiana or were deported back to France. Astonishingly, like migratory birds or butterflies, quite a number of surviving Acadians (some had died during deportation) managed to return a decade or so later, sometimes to the same plot of land they had been forced to abandon. As Henry Wadsworth Longfellow writes, in his famous Acadian-based poem *Evangeline*, they returned to "the shore of the mournful and misty Atlantic," having journeyed "back to their native land."

The oysters they had harvested, and continued to harvest in Canadian waters, had of course remained and were once again lovingly gathered, and eventually farmed as well.

An Acadian oyster, therefore, calls forth intriguingly complicated emotions. Whether it be a Malpeque from Prince Edward Island, a Beausoleil from New Brunswick's

Miramichi Bay, or the famed Caraquet from the south side of Chaleur Bay, it will always telegraph a beautiful forlornness because of its associations with banishment and exile. Both lyrical and sharply defined, these oysters have a rich, savoury narrative, one that lingers long in the memory and insists upon return. Swallowing an Acadian oyster is like ingesting an aria: it brings tears to the eyes.

The Acadians themselves are quick to point out the symbolism of these northern beauties. While the oysters of the lands of banishment—Louisiana and other southern parts of North America—have succumbed to the effects of pollution, those of the cherished northern homeland have flourished and are now sought after as delicacies all over the continent, long after the colonial wars—and the upheaval and sorrow they brought with them—have all but vanished from our collective memory.

Temple

U NTIL RELATIVELY RECENTLY, DRIVING ON Highway 427 north of Toronto's Pearson Airport has had little to recommend it. One container building follows after another on this freeway, along with other forms of uninteresting industrial architecture of various species, all squatting under a roaring, contrail-filled sky. It is a land of concrete, asphalt, and aluminum siding. One wants to get away from there as soon as possible. As if intuiting this, and with a stunning lack of irony, the Ontario government has placed on this stretch an official Ministry of Transportation sign announcing that Algonquin Park, with its iconic rocks and lakes, is only 257 kilometres to the north. Under the circumstances, this is almost impossible to believe.

Then suddenly, a large, glowing palace-like structure of extraordinary loveliness presents itself in one's line of vision, so "other" and serene, so wonderfully rendered that

214

the experience is close to hallucinatory. This is the BAPS Shri Swaminarayan Mandir, a Hindu temple built using Indian, Italian, and Turkish marble, during the first decade of the twenty-first century, in the centre of what might otherwise have remained simply a grey expanse of industrial wasteland. Assembled according to the rules of sacred architecture and surrounded by eighteen acres of gardens, the temple comprises twenty-four thousand parts—each one representing a Hindu god or goddess and hand-carved in one of the many Indian villages that worked on the project.

Hindus have been in Canada for about one hundred years. In the beginning, their numbers were small and almost all lived in British Columbia. Now they number half a million, and nearly three-quarters live in Ontario. BAPS Shri Swaminarayan Mandir provides not only a place of worship and spiritual contemplation but also a cultural centre, educational facility, and residential home for dozens of graceful, orange-robed sadhus (monks). Among the sadhus' duties is the overseeing of sacred rituals, including the clothing and bathing of images of the deities, which are viewed as embodying the divine. Festivals are held, languages are taught, musical concerts take place, and everything in the vicinity is a feast for the eyes. There is a museum on the grounds, and in the spirit of education and inclusiveness, the temple itself is open to visitors.

Over eighteen hundred artisans worked on carving the

twenty-four thousand statues. One can imagine these carvers in their far-off villages, focused on their faith and their art, utterly unaware of the physical and spiritual blankness of the surroundings their work would so stirringly enhance. Even glimpsed from a distance, the Mandir is a wonder, an enormous gift, not only to the Toronto Indo-Canadian Hindu community but to Canada as a whole.

Table

THE TABLE I AM WORKING ON RIGHT NOW IS twelve feet long and four feet wide. It is made from two long pine boards, the widest of which is two and a half feet. Both pieces of timber must have come from among the first forests Europeans encountered in the New World, those mysterious and now lost Carolinian mixed woodlands that grew in what we now call Ontario, Quebec, and upstate New York. Sadly, finding a one-and-a-half-foot board these days is unlikely, and finding one two and a half feet wide is impossible.

This simple but beautiful piece of furniture was made to be the council table for elected representatives of Cramahe Township, and was situated, therefore, in the council chambers of Castleton's town hall. The town hall itself was built in 1893, but I would say, based on the size of the boards, that the table predates the building that once housed it by quite a number of years, and perhaps occupied a previous pioneer meeting hall where the affairs of the new township were discussed. Whatever the case, I am lucky enough to work on such a splendid table-scape because in 1970, my father, having heard that the table was being replaced, made arrangements to rescue it and to transport it to his own study. For him, it made a wonderful surface for laying out maps. For me, it is the perfect spot to both write and do research at the same time.

Early furniture in Canada varied from makeshift to masterful, and was made of materials ranging from the simple but stunning pine boards of Cramahe's council table to glowing French-polished mahogany. When Queen Elizabeth II came to Canada in 1982 to sign the Royal Proclamation of the Constitution Act, which would give Canada the right to amend its own Constitution, a lovely, small table was brought outdoors from the Senate Speaker's suite on Parliament Hill. No one seems certain of how the table originally came to be in the Speaker's suite, but with its hoofed feet, perfectly square top, and expertly turned central pedestal, it was deemed suitable to support the royal arm and the royal signing hand.

There is some suggestion that the wood of what would come to be called the Constitution Table comes from more than one place, making the piece, like the country in which it was constructed, a sort of hybrid. Parts of its structure

are fabricated with pine, while others—the haunches supporting the top, for example—are believed to be walnut. The warm colour of the actual tabletop, however, has led some to insist that it is made of mahogany imported from the Caribbean at the request of Quebec cabinetmakers, who were highly skilled when it came to working with this valuable wood.

The Constitution Act, with its Canadian Charter of Rights and Freedoms, not only made Canada independent of Britain, but also went a considerable distance toward ensuring equality for all Canadians.

Burnt Mask

I N THE ROYAL BRITISH COLUMBIA MUSEUM IN
Victoria, there is an important piece of what the curator
calls "museum theatre." A reconstructed Haisla mask,
partly burnt, lies beside the following statement made by a
Kitamaat woman:

> *My grandmother told me that when Christianity came
> her uncle went down to the beach and burned every-
> thing. He had heard that the Lord will not receive you if
> you still look to your treasures.*

ACKNOWLEDGEMENTS

THIS BOOK WOULD NOT HAVE BEEN POSSIBLE WITH-out a great deal of help and advice from people all across Canada. In fact, the generosity and openness of the individuals that Scott McKowen and I sought out, or, in some cases, came across in our research, says something very affirming about the country as a whole. People were eager to share their experiences, their culture, their expertise, and their time with us. Their enthusiasms became our enthusiasms. We are grateful to them all.

Our heartfelt thanks to Christina Poddubiuk, Allysha Witt, Grace Laemmler, Stratford-Perth Archives, Carol and Bob Passmore, Elizabeth Davidson, Mieke Bevelander, Marianne Brandis, Mark Poddubiuk, Niagara Historical Museum in Niagara-on-the-Lake, Dr. Martha Black at the Royal British Columbia Museum, Michael Wagner, Jeremy Ward at the Canadian Canoe Museum, Heather Bradley, Liza

225

Giffen at the Stratford Festival Archives, David Cooper, Sam Ennis, the L.M. Montgomery Collection at the University of Guelph Library, Michael Ondaatje, Ken Nutt, Daniel Sharp at the Visual Art Collection of the Canadian Department of Foreign Affairs, Haroon Siddiqui, Alice Munro, Ontario Jewish Archives, Jan Ross of the Emily Carr House in Victoria, Rochel Urist, Baltej Dhillon, Ric Heinl of George Heinl and Company, Timothy Bergen, Anne Chafe of The Rooms Provincial Museum in Newfoundland, Himy Syed, Susan Swan, Pat Martin Bates, Mathieu Drouin of Musée des Ursulines de Québec, Brent Michaluk and Jacqueline Kirk of the CBC, Charlotte Gray, the Ontario Jewish Archives, David Morrison at the Canadian Museum of History, Ariel Rogers at Fogarty's Cove Music, Andrew Trant, Nick Carter, Lawrence Hill, Michael Phillips, Tony Urquhart, David Thauberger, Shane O'Dea, Sandra Martin, Roger Hall, Gabrielle Israelievitch, Jim Polk, and the late Cliff Quinn.

Heartfelt thanks also to editor and publisher Patrick Crean for coming up with the idea for this project, and for advice and support during its execution. We are also grateful to senior vice-president and executive publisher Iris Tupholme, managing editorial director Noelle Zitzer, and everyone else on the team at HarperCollins. I personally owe a special debt of gratitude to Janice Weaver for her patient and assiduous copy edit: there were many instances when she saved me from myself.

Thank you to the countless others who provided information, directions, advice, sympathy, suggestions, thoughts, and excitement. This book is for you.